THE ANCIENT SOUTHWEST

& Other Dispatches from a Cruel Frontier

ALSO BY PRICE & TURNER

The Cinema of Adventure, Romance & Terror

The Southwest Heritage Series

The Making of King Kong (with Dr. Orville Goldner)

Murder in the Palo Duro & Other Panhandle Mysteries

Spawn of Skull Island

Forgotten Horrors, Volumes 1-4 (with John Wooley)

Human Monsters: The Bizarre Psychology of Movie Villains

Human Monsters: The Definitive Edition

Roy Crane, the collected Wash Tubbs & Captain Easy

Al Capp, the collected Li'l Abner

V.T. Hamlin, the collected Alley Oop

Stan Lynde, the collected Rick O'Shay

The Spider

Southern-Fried Homicide

Muñeca

Holiday for Screams

Fisherman's Laugh Book

THE ANCIENT SOUTHWEST

& OTHER DISPATCHES FROM A CRUEL FRONTIER

MICHAEL H. PRICE · GEORGE E. TURNER

FOREWORD BY ARTHUR B. BUSBEY

TCU Press
Fort Worth

Library of Congress Cataloging-in-Publication Data

Turner, George, 1925-
The Ancient Southwest & other dispatches from a cruel frontier /
Michael H. Price, George E. Turner; foreword by Arthur B. Busbey.
p. cm.
Collection of George Turner's comic strips which originally appeared
in The Sunday news-globe of Amarillo, Texas.
ISBN 0-87565-306-5 (pbk. : alk. paper)
1. Southwest, New—Discovery and exploration—Caricatures and
cartoons. 2. Núñez Cabeza de Vaca, Alvar, 16th cent.—Caricatures and
cartoons. 3. Southwest, New—Antiquities—Caricatures and cartoons. 4.
Southwest, New—History—Caricatures and cartoons. 5. Frontier and pioneer
life—Southwest, New—Caricatures and cartoons. 6. Palo Duro Canyon
(Tex.)—Discovery and exploration—Caricatures and cartoons. 7. Palo
Duro Canyon (Tex.)—Antiquities—Caricatures and cartoons. 8. Palo Duro
Canyon (Tex.)—History—Caricatures and cartoons. I. Title: Ancient
Southwest and other dispatches from a cruel frontier. II. Price, Michael
H., 1947- III. Title.
F799.T87 2005
917.9—dc22

Printed in Canada

200402678

for
CHRISTINA RENTERIA PRICE
and
JEAN WADE TURNER

CONTENTS

FOREWORD

By Arthur B. Busbey

This somewhat eclectic collection of George E. Turner's cartoons contains his series of educational cartoons, as well as cartoons that document his growth as an artist. Turner's "historical/educational" cartoons put the gleam in my eye and serve as the focus of my comments. Turner's cartoons interest me as a scientist because they represent an entertaining and, I think, successful attempt to transfer knowledge from the technical realm of academia to the everyday realm of the "public."

Pushing scientific information through the science/generalist sieve is never easy and can be conceptually messy. In any gathering of scientists, when the conversation turns to science and the general public, we frequently admonish ourselves for doing a haphazard job of communicating scientific knowledge to the public. Yet, a scientifically literate public is critical for informed public decisions. Frequently, the public knows little about science other than "sound bites" or newspaper fillers that may flash through the consciousness while a reader tears through the morning paper or listens, half-heartedly, to news reports that, themselves, half-heartedly present the "news." In the last twenty to thirty years, more attempts at scientific outreach have been made than in the long history of science. Most of these attempts have been greatly aided by the new venues of mass communication.

Unfortunately, in the attempt to entertain and educate a typical scientifically "sub-literate" public, the focus frequently falls on entertainment rather than on education. So-called science series and television specials happily mix mythology and science and frequently twist the facts to give the science a "Wow!" appeal. Unfortunately, the science may get so twisted that it no longer resembles what scientists think of as science. An even balance must be achieved between the visual impact of entertainment and the intellectual impact of science.

Dynamic though modern visual-arts approaches to science education are, they are ultimately the descendants of early attempts at "science" education. These geological and historical cartoons represent an early attempt to educate the public about distant history in a popular medium that stimulates the imagination while it promotes the distribution of useful scientific knowledge. Perhaps these vignettes are in the style of *Alley Oop*, but they present scholarly knowledge in digestible form. They still manage to elicit a "Wow!" response that is just as genuine today as it was in the middle of the twentieth century when the series was published. Turner's collaboration with Dr. Roy Reinhart, as edited by Michael Price for the present collection, resulted in a wealthy public depository of information about the pre- and European history of Texas and the Southwest.

What pleased the eye over fifty years ago is still compelling. If you can forgive wisecracking dinosaurs and a strange assortment of bathing beauties (appreciate them as visual iconographies of contemporary mid-twentieth-century popular culture), you will see a series of comics that provide windows into lost times and places. Though half a century old, the cartoons still evoke a sense of wonder as they lead the reader through an exploration of the both the geology and the European conquest of what we now call Texas. In them you learn of the earliest Texans, some of whom were quite scaly, and our more immediate Native American and European predecessors.

Many of the facts that these comics introduced have not changed. The organisms that Turner had pictured are still found in the rocks of Texas, although since the 1950s many more fossil species have been found. Most of the names of animals you see in these comics also appear in modern catalogs of the fossils of Texas. Although the way in which we interpret some of the science and the history has changed, time has not dimmed the basic facts.

Sit back, open the book, and soak up a liberal broth of the ancient history of Texas.

—Arthur B. Busbey
TCU
November 2004

INTRODUCTION

By Michael H. Price

George E. Turner (1925-1999) launched his first earnest attempt at a comic strip early in 1951 under a title that wavered between *The Ancient Southwest* and *The Ancient Great Plains*—continuity depending, no doubt, upon which editor might be ramrodding any given edition. George's venue was the Amarillo, Texas, *Sunday News-Globe*, the weekend showcase publication of a self-contained group of daily newspapers whose circulation spanned Northwest Texas and reached well into Oklahoma, Kansas, New Mexico and Colorado.

The artist and cultural historian Stephen R. Bissette, whose *Tyrant* books of the 1990s cover a great deal of prehistoric ground, has appraised *The Ancient Southwest* in these terms: "Turner undertook nothing less than a painstakingly illustrated science comic strip detailing the evolution of life in his home state, rich with the myriad forms of flora and fauna that swam, slithered, stalked and soared across millions of years. . . . This is, very likely, the first true American dinosaur comic."[1] (And yes, Vincent Trout Hamlin's *Alley Oop* patently had enjoyed a generation's head start at depicting dinosaurs in comic-strip panels; Hamlin's concerns lay more in science fiction than in pure science, however, and *Oop*'s dinosaurs served more of a supporting function.)

George's collaborator on *The Ancient Southwest*, for a short while, was Dr. Roy H. Reinhart, a professor of geology at West Texas State College (now

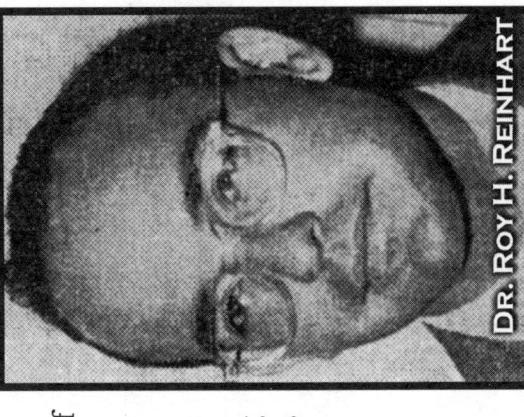

DR. ROY H. REINHART

GEORGE E. TURNER

West Texas A&M University) at Canyon. Their weekly strip was business as usual for Reinhart—a singularly gifted scholar, capable of transforming complex scientific information into memorable and entertaining lectures and monographs—but it represented a modest breakthrough for George, who recently had returned to his native Texas following studies at the Art Institute of Chicago and the American Academy of Art. George was in the process of establishing a studio and gallery while settling in as a technical illustrator at Amarillo Air Force Base and moonlighting as a production designer and calligrapher at the printing shop of Russell Stationery Company.

The Ancient Southwest was a popular success from the start, even drawing out one intensely responsive crackpot from among the local readership and thus provoking a running controversy that provided some additional entertainment value beyond the province of the feature itself.

George based a promotional advertisement on a scene from *The Lost World*, a 1925-vintage motion picture that had paved the way for the 1933 *King Kong*. The influence of *King Kong*, in its turn, had set George as a child upon a pastime-as-career path from which he never would veer, combining such interests as imaginative fiction and heroic adventure, Real World paleontology, fine art and commercial illustration, and moviemaking techniques and technologies. It comes scarcely as a surprise to notice that the mighty Kong himself puts in a guest appearance in *The Ancient Southwest*.

George also was springing from an admiration of the daily strip, *Alley Oop*. V.T. Hamlin's cavemen-and-dinosaurs fantasies, inspired by direct observa-

Above: *The series-launching advertisement*

tions of the natural history of Texas during the 1920s as an illustrator with the *Star-Telegram* of Fort Worth, had become a staple of the Amarillo newspapers, among many others. George found additional motivation in Charles R. Knight's celebrated paintings of pre-antiquity as it must have been and in the research into prehistory of Dr. Roy Chapman Andrews.

An announcement in *The Prairie*, the weekly newspaper of West Texas State College, declared, "Dr. Reinhart emphasizes that these strips are being done to increase popular geological interest."[2] And how better to do so, than with a discreet measure of sensationalism?

George Turner, though already a fixture of the community and a respected voice in its academic sector, also indulged a prankish sense of humor. During this period, George perpetrated one of the finer repercussive stunts in the history of West Texas State College. One day while visiting the campus' Panhandle-Plains Historical Museum (where Dr. Reinhart served as a curator), George and fellow illustrator Gene A. Clardy were heading toward the main galleries when it occurred to George that they had neglected to sign the guest register. Duly returning to the entrance, where a uniformed guard sat absorbed in a magazine, they approached the massive leather-bound volume. Giving in to a momentary impulse, George signed a letter-perfect forgery of a famous signature: Norman Rockwell.

Whereupon Turner and Clardy went on about their tour. "We were puttering about the cowboy exhibits," George recalled, many years later. "We'd completely forgotten about my casual act of forgery—when here comes a-running the chairman of the historical society, all dithered up. 'Have you seen him?' he asks

Above: Turner's campus-newspaper cartoons often traded on such pop-cultural icons as Al Capp's comic strip, Li'l Abner. (Capp's Sadie Hawkins Day was a husband-capturing tournament.)

Gene and me. 'Seen whom?' says Gene. 'Why, Norman Rockwell,' says the Big Cheese. 'He's right here—in our own museum. Signed in, just as sure as you're born, not an hour ago.'"[3]

George continued: "'Well, no, sir,' says I, 'and I'd certainly think Norman Rockwell would be a difficult guy to miss noticing. *Uhm*—we'll be watching, yessir.'

"'This is our most important visit since the governor,' says the chairman, 'and I've already alerted the press. So they'll be right out. You boys keep an eye peeled, now, won't you?'

"'Oh, we'll keep a lookout, all right,' says Gene, jabbing me in the ribs with his elbow. Which meant the time was right for us to vamoose out of there. Which we did—just in time to see the newspaper and radio guys, and the president of the college, Dr. [James P.] Cornette, and that big-shot rancher, J. Evetts Haley, who was known as the 'phantom president' of WTSC, on account of his strong-arm influence. And, of course, they all knew me, what with my diploma from that cherished institution and my ties to the newspaper. And Gene and I just kept on a-movin'.

"It was all over the papers and the radio, next day, about the 'visit' from the Great Man,"[4] George continued. "Somebody had finally thought to place a call to Norman Rockwell's studio—and determined right off that he was nowhere within shouting distance of the Texas Panhandle, except by telephone. It was a great story, of the non-story variety. Gene's and my role in it would've made it an even keener non-story, but we kept mum. I mean, for *years* we kept mum."[5]

George and Dr. Reinhart had a local hit on their hands from the beginning of *The Ancient Southwest*, but the Globe-News Publishing Company neglected to seize its potential for syndication, not even bothering to share the feature with a kindred publication in nearby Lubbock. A vigorous letters-to-the-editor response found the more wide-awake readers likening George's artwork to the Charles R. Knight paintings in Chicago's Field Museum and inquiring, "Could you give it more space?"[6]

One reader, however, launched an impassioned if half-baked tirade that threatened to become a series in its own right: "None can with impunity question [the strip's] statistics or factual data," wrote Benjamin Max Franklin of Amarillo, "but [the] conclusions that the animals roamed these Plains and the fish swam these seas are based on rate of erosion, rate and method of strata-forming, and rate of evolution, the true factors of which [Dr. Reinhart] has not the slightest glimmering."[7]

Franklin continued: "The facts are: (1) None of the animals lived here, they were merely buried here. (2) The guiding factors by which the date or time or age are determined are not yet known. Dr. Reinhart's million [years] could be a thousand or a billion. ... Hope you either change these comic strips or else refuse to present them as factual or near-factual."[8]

Over the course of his correspondence, the indignant Mr. Franklin asserted a case for a non-rotating earth, whose spinning would finally have begun "in historic times." As to the scarcity of signs of early humankind, Franklin pointed to indications "only that [man] was able to escape the floods or . . . lived in an area that was not subject to the most violent floods."[9] Then the tirades stopped as abruptly as they had begun. The feature continued into 1952.

In late 1951, Dr. Reinhart left Texas for a faculty post with Miami University at Oxford, Ohio.[10] George carried on as writer-and-illustrator, keeping the feature rooted in science but becoming ever more adventurous in its presentation. (Reinhart found greater prominence as a geologist and paleontologist; his discovery of a well-preserved femur from a prehistoric elephant is a fixture at Miami University's Hefner Zoological Museum.) In 1952, *Amateur Art & Camera* magazine devoted an elaborate article to *The Ancient Southwest*, describing George's

Above: Turner's sketches, circa 1950, in search of a logotype for his gallery-studio; finished design on the following page.

savvy use of photographs and relics as reference models and hailing his ambitious expansion from newspaper cartooning into books and magazines.[11] George halted the strip that year to launch a more expansive comic feature called *The Palo Duro Story*, also for the *Sunday News-Globe*, relating the Spanish invasion of the New World from, largely, the assumed point of view of the explorer Álvar Núñez Cabeza de Vaca. *The Palo Duro Story* ends rather awkwardly--right at the start of a new episode involving a search for the fabled Golden City of Cibola--as a consequence of George's increasing duties as a general-purpose illustrator with the newspapers. George returned to the topic in a loose-knit series of lavishly illustrated text features for the *Sunday News-Globe*, but only as deadlines permitted.

George was gradually insinuating himself into a full-time art directorship within the Amarillo papers' newsroom, where he felt more comfortable than he had among the United States Air Force bureaucrats or within West Texas' small-but-stuffy society of artists, with its sternly drawn lines between Art-with-a-capital-A and cartooning.

These early comic features had established George as a popular storyteller, even without the prestige or the wider recognition of syndication. The Globe-News Publishing Company and its successor, the Georgia-based Morris Communications Corporation, provided George with a practical base of operations, however confining, for many years to follow.

During the 1960s, George also became a founding editor and publisher of *Southwest Heritage* magazine; he sold his interest in that scholarly journal in 1969 but continued to write and draw for it after its absorption into *Grain Producers News*, a magazine published by Amarillo-based Producers Grain Corporation for its employees and its clients.

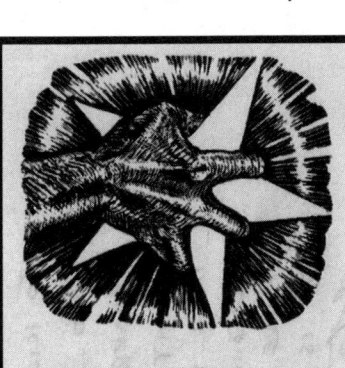

"Dedicated to the preservation of sanity in Art"

Amarillo Academy of Art

George E. Turner Studio

720 W. 10th, Apt. 4   Phone 3-8027

Amarillo, Texas

George finally pulled up stakes in 1978 for a career switch to the motion-picture industry in Los Angeles. There, he carried on as a storyboard-and-effects artist for such filmmakers as Francis Ford Coppola and Carl Reiner, as editor of *The American Cinematographer* magazine, and as resident historian of the American Society of Cinematographers.

In addition to such duties and the continuing workload of a collaborative series of movie-history books that he and I had launched in 1975, George worked in cartoon animation and as a contributing researcher with both the Academy of Motion Picture Arts & Sciences and the American Film Institute. He had become a storyboard artist and second-unit director with the network television series *Friends* shortly before his unexpected death at age seventy-three.

Both *The Ancient Southwest* and *The Palo Duro Story* are reproduced here in toto as a sustained body of work from a promising new talent, as restored and revised during 1999-2005 by Yours Truly—something of a coda to my lengthy working relationship with George Turner. (George had nurtured the hope of republishing these features as late as 1999, but he found the prospect of a restoration project intimidating in the absence of the original artwork. The present overhaul uses a combination of newsprint tearsheets, retouching and re-inking, and digital imaging.) A sampling of strips from *The Ancient Southwest* also can be found in their unembellished original form in the book *Spawn of Skull Island* (Baltimore: Luminary Press, 2002), my posthumous revision of George's watershed volume of motion-picture history, *The Making of King Kong* (London and Cranbury, N.J.: The Tantivy Press and A.S. Barnes & Company, 1975). For the present book's closing section, I have retrieved from George's files a generous if random selection of seldom-seen schoolboy, collegiate and professional efforts, ranging from circa 1940 into the 1960s. Even the more overtly humorous specimens among the earlier work foreshadow in many particulars the interests and the style that George brought to bear on *The Ancient Southwest* and *The Palo Duro Story*.

—MICHAEL H. PRICE
Somewhere between the Llano
Estacádo and Vásquez Rocks

NOTES

1 Stephen R. Bissette, "The Paleo Path," in Jim Lawson's *The Collected Paleo: Tales of the Late Cretaceous* (Haydenville, Massachusetts: ZeroMayo Studios, 2003), pp. 2-3.

2 "Cartoon Starts in *News-Globe*," *The Prairie*, student newspaper of West Texas State College at Canyon, February 16, 1951, p. 1.

3 George Turner's reference is to Harold Dow Bugbee (1900-1963), the acclaimed western artist and historian, who also served at the time as the museum's curator of art.

4 "Norman Rockwell Visits Canyon's Museum—or Does He?" Amarillo [Texas] *Daily News*, March 15, 1951, p. 1.

5 From an audiotape recording of a conversation with George E. Turner; Amarillo, September-October, 1975. Archives of the author.

6 "Preening Our Feathers," Letters to the Editor: Tri-State Forum, Amarillo *Daily News*, May 15, 1951, p. 16.

7 "Comic Strip Debate," Letters to the Editor: Tri-State Forum, Amarillo *Daily News*, May 19, 1951, p. 20.

8 Ibid.

9 "Scientific Approach," Letters to the Editor: Tri-State Forum, Amarillo *Daily News*, June 5, 1951, p. 18.

10 "Geology Professor at WT Resigns Post," *The Times* of Amarillo, December 6, 1951; "Dr. Roy Reinhart Resigns WT Job," Amarillo *Globe*, December 7, 1951.

11 "Photo Studies Aid Cartoonists," *Amateur Art & Camera* magazine, January 1952, pp. 20-21.

THE ANCIENT SOUTHWEST

THE ANCIENT SOUTHWEST

BY M.H. PRICE & GEORGE E. TURNER

Mr. Luther Joe Pybus, of Amarillo, writes in with a compelling question:

"WERE THE HORSES BROUGHT TO THE SOUTHWEST BY THE SPANISH CONQUERORS THE FIRST EVER TO BE SEEN BY THE INDIANS?"

Good question, too — so good, that the jury's still out on it. But yes, the modern breeds were introduced from the so-called "Old World." And yet, the earliest known prehistoric horses originated here.

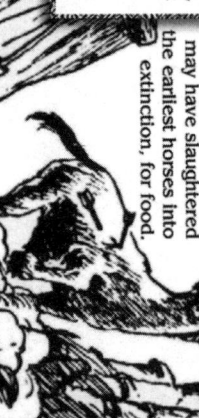

The earliest Americans may have slaughtered the earliest horses into extinction, for food.

It seems unlikely that horses were ever used as beasts of burden by the American Indians prior to the reintroduction from Europe.

THE ANCIENT SOUTHWEST

BY M.H. PRICE & GEORGE E. TURNER

THE TRILOBITE, ONE OF THE EARLIEST FORMS OF LIFE, IS NOW REPRESENTED BY MANY DESCENDANTS COMMONLY SEEN DURING PICNIC SEASON.

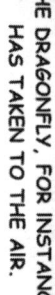

THE DRAGONFLY, FOR INSTANCE, HAS TAKEN TO THE AIR.

THE CRAYFISH — SOME FOLKS CALL IT A CRAWDAD — REMAINS LOYAL TO ITS WATERY ORIGINS...

... WHILE THE CENTIPEDE IS AS TRUE AN EVOLUTIONARY THROW-BACK AS CAN BE FOUND.

THE ANCIENT SOUTHWEST

By M.H. Price & George E. Turner

SCORPIONS WERE PROBABLY THE FIRST AIR-BREATHING ANIMALS TO LEAVE THE ANCIENT SEAS.

THE FORERUNNERS OF THE SCORPIONS WERE SHALLOW-WATER SEA-DWELLERS KNOWN AS EURYPTERIDS. THEY PUT IN THEIR APPEARANCE ABOUT 390 MILLION YEARS AGO (THE SILURIAN PERIOD, IN CASE ANYONE WAS WONDERING).

TRACES OF THESE ANCIENT "SEA SCORPIONS" ARE SOMETIMES FOUND TO MEASURE AS MUCH AS 10 FEET IN LENGTH.

THE ANCIENT SOUTHWEST

By M.H. Price & George E. Turner

IF IT WERE POSSIBLE TO DROP A BAITED HOOK INTO THE SEAS THAT ONCE COVERED THE SOUTH-WESTERN PLAINS — ALL OF 330 MILLION YEARS AGO, THAT IS...

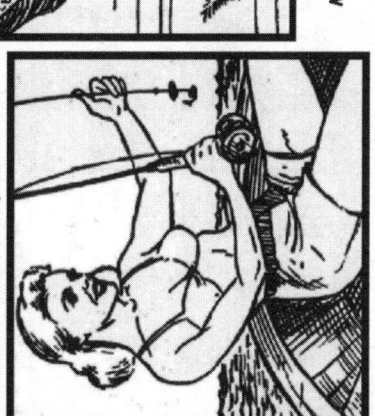

... ONE MIGHT CATCH ALL MANNER OF WEIRD ARMOR-PLATED FISH.

PERHAPS IT IS BETTER THAT SUCH IS IMPOSSIBLE...

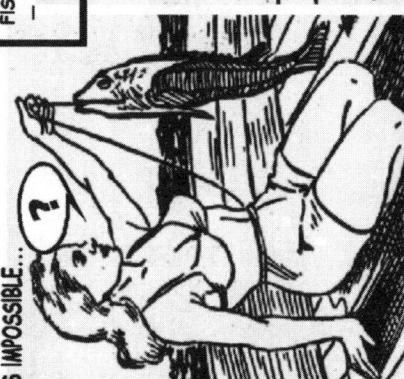

... FOR ONE OF THE LARGER SUCH FISH — SAY, THE 20-FOOT DINICHTYHS — WOULD BE LIKELY AS NOT TO MAKE A MEAL OF ANY ANGLER.

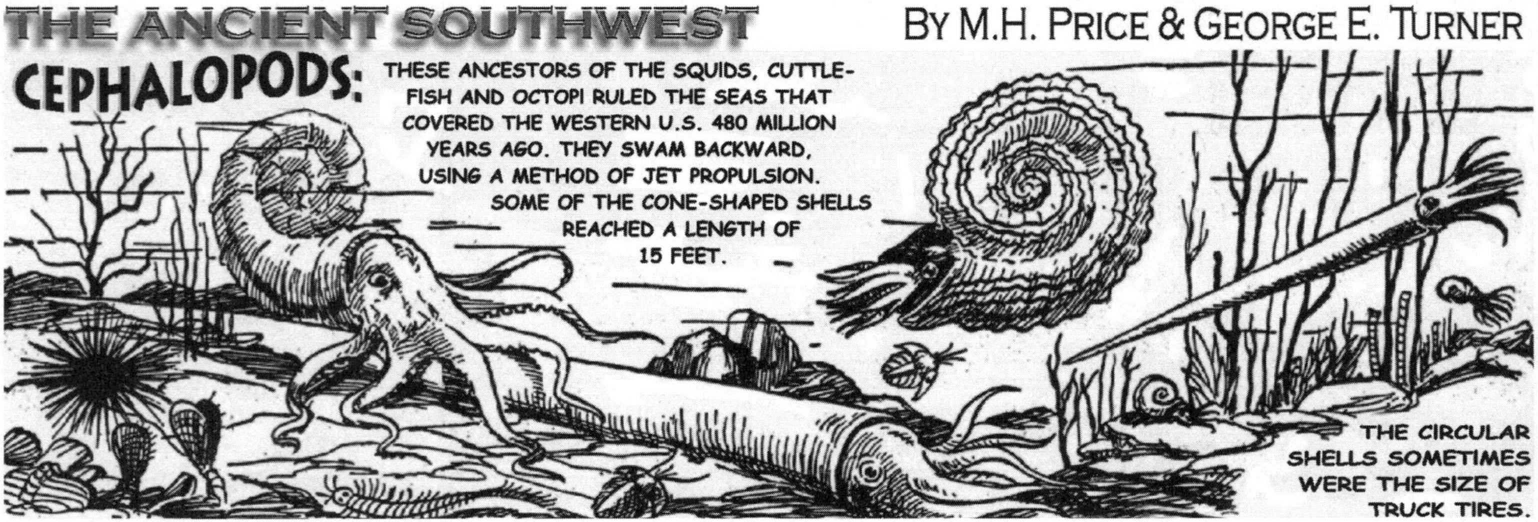
THE ANCIENT SOUTHWEST
BY M.H. PRICE & GEORGE E. TURNER
CEPHALOPODS:
THESE ANCESTORS OF THE SQUIDS, CUTTLE-FISH AND OCTOPI RULED THE SEAS THAT COVERED THE WESTERN U.S. 480 MILLION YEARS AGO. THEY SWAM BACKWARD, USING A METHOD OF JET PROPULSION. SOME OF THE CONE-SHAPED SHELLS REACHED A LENGTH OF 15 FEET.
THE CIRCULAR SHELLS SOMETIMES WERE THE SIZE OF TRUCK TIRES.

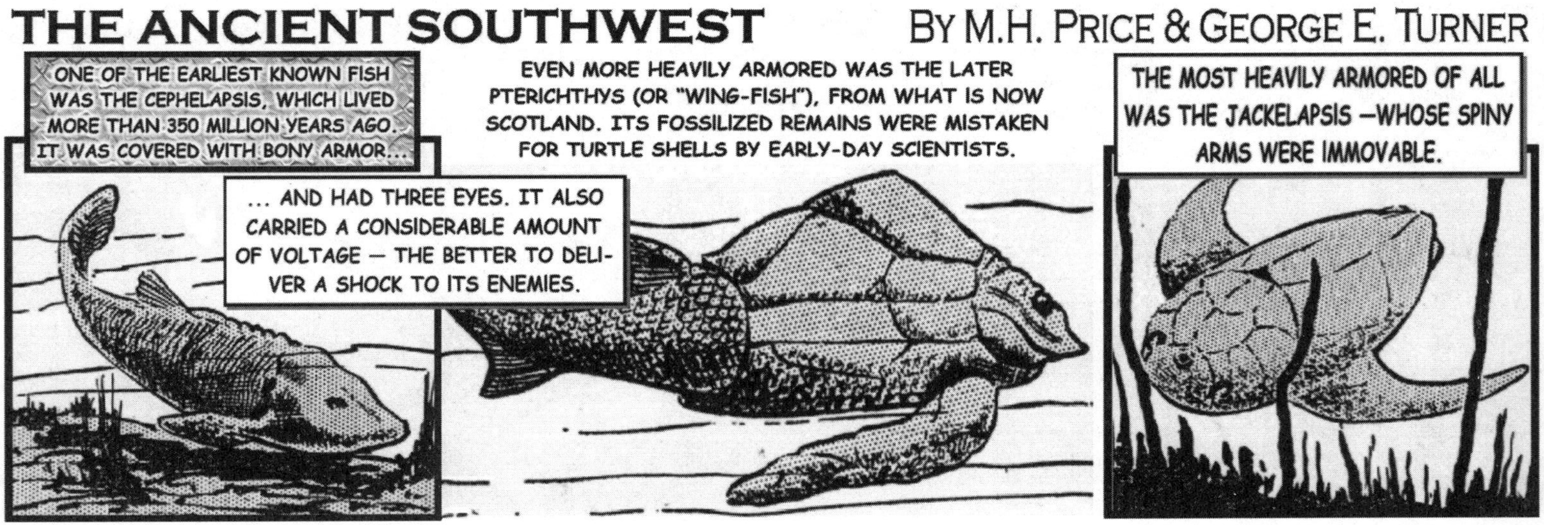
THE ANCIENT SOUTHWEST
BY M.H. PRICE & GEORGE E. TURNER
ONE OF THE EARLIEST KNOWN FISH WAS THE CEPHELAPSIS, WHICH LIVED MORE THAN 350 MILLION YEARS AGO. IT WAS COVERED WITH BONY ARMOR...
... AND HAD THREE EYES. IT ALSO CARRIED A CONSIDERABLE AMOUNT OF VOLTAGE — THE BETTER TO DELIVER A SHOCK TO ITS ENEMIES.
EVEN MORE HEAVILY ARMORED WAS THE LATER PTERICHTHYS (OR "WING-FISH"), FROM WHAT IS NOW SCOTLAND. ITS FOSSILIZED REMAINS WERE MISTAKEN FOR TURTLE SHELLS BY EARLY-DAY SCIENTISTS.
THE MOST HEAVILY ARMORED OF ALL WAS THE JACKELAPSIS —WHOSE SPINY ARMS WERE IMMOVABLE.

THE ANCIENT SOUTHWEST

By M.H. Price & George E. Turner

FROM THE GREAT COAL AGE OF 250 MILLION YEARS AGO.

ERYOPS

THIS MONSTER AMPHIBIAN WAS NEARLY 10 FEET IN LENGTH. IT HAD THREE EYES AND A VOICE WITH WHICH TO CROAK. THIS DISTINCTION IS IMPORTANT, AS NO EARLIER KNOWN ANIMAL POSSESSED A VOCAL MECHANISM.

THE LARGEST BULLFROGS ON RECORD HAVE WEIGHED AS MUCH AS 3.5 POUNDS. SUCH WORTHY SPECIMENS ARE HARDLY BIGGER THAN ONE OF THE WARTS COVERING THE BACK OF SOME OF THE ANCIENT TEXAS FROG ANCESTORS, SUCH AS...

THE ANCIENT SOUTHWEST

By M.H. Price & George E. Turner

THE **ANGLE**-HEADED *DIPLOCAULUS*
... PROBABLY LOOKED SOME-

THING LIKE THIS AS IT SWAM ABOUT THE CARBON-LADEN SWAMPS OF 250 MILLION YEARS AGO.

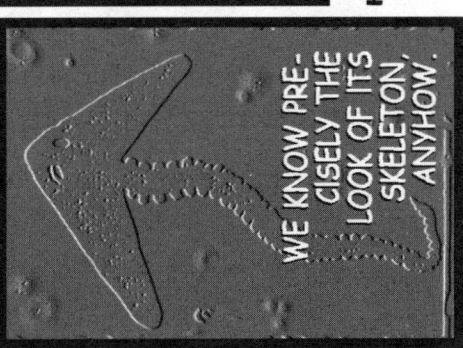

WE KNOW PRE-CISELY THE LOOK OF ITS SKELETON, ANYHOW.

INFANTS OF THE SPECIES HAD MORE OF A ROUNDED SKULL. THE ARROWHEAD SHAPE APPARENTLY DE-VELOPED WITH GROWTH.

THE ANCIENT SOUTHWEST

By M.H. Price & George E. Turner

THE CRINOIDS THRIVED DURING THE TIMES WHEN THE MISSISSIPPIAN SEAS COVERED NORTH AMERICA — THEIR FOSSILS ARE ABUNDANT BECAUSE THE CREATURES WERE COVERED WITH LIME. THIS ROCK IS MADE UP OF *THOUSANDS* OF CRINOID FOSSILS!

MANY A TRIBAL PRINCESS HAS WORN BEADS MADE OF FOSSILIZED CRINOIDS, OR "SEA LILIES" —ACTUALLY, ANIMAL LIFE DATING FROM 300 MILLION YEARS AGO.

THEY LOOK LIKE STARFISH — GROWING ON A STEM, LIKE FLOWERS!

THESE STRANGE, FRAGILE ANIMALS WERE THE NATURAL PREY OF PREHISTORIC SHARKS.

THE ANCIENT SOUTHWEST

By M.H. Price & George E. Turner

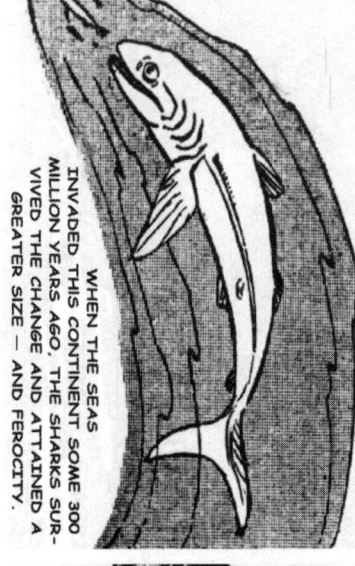

THE EARLY SHARKS, OF WHICH THIS *CLADESOLACHE* WAS TYPICAL, WERE FRESH-WATER FISH INHABITING THE RIVERS. THE LARGER ONES WERE SCARCELY THREE FEET LONG.

WHEN THE SEAS INVADED THIS CONTINENT SOME 300 MILLION YEARS AGO, THE SHARKS SURVIVED THE CHANGE AND ATTAINED A GREATER SIZE — AND FEROCITY.

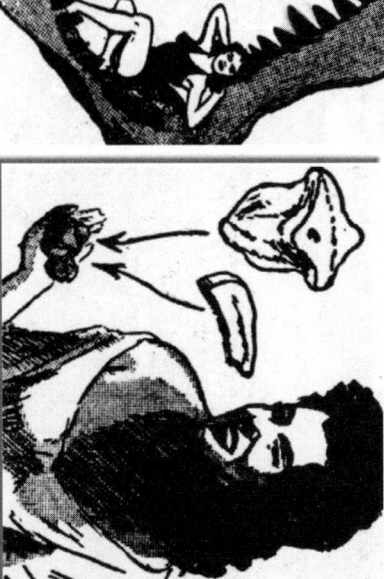

IN NUMBERS, TOO, THE SHARKS OUTCLASSED ALL OTHER SEA BEASTS. THE JAWS SHOWN HERE BELONG TO A SHARK OF THE MISSISSIPPIAN PERIOD.

NOT ALL THE SHARKS WERE TEARERS OF FLESH. SOME HAD FLAT, CRUSHING TEETH TO CRACK THE SHELLS OF THEIR PREY.

THE ANCIENT SOUTHWEST

BY M.H. PRICE & GEORGE E. TURNER

Some of us might suspect that the oldest eggs in the world are the work of teevee gagwriters.

YEP — AND THANK GOODNESS FOR CANNED LAUGHTER!

UH-HYUCK!

But the fossilized dinosaur eggs found during a 20th Century U.S. expedition to Mongolia are vastly older — and almost as well known.

Texas, however, is the source of the most ancient known egg — about 225 million years old, thus out-dating the Mongolian eggs by more than 100 million years. Here is the native proto-Texan believed to have left the egg:

Science calls this six-foot beauty by a mouthful of a name:

OPHIACODON

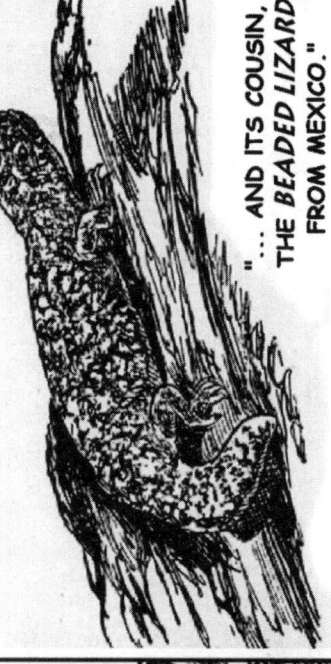

THE ANCIENT SOUTHWEST

BY M.H. PRICE & GEORGE E. TURNER

"YOUR CONCERN IS TOUCHING, BUT THERE AREN'T ANY POISONOUS LIZARDS IN THESE PARTS — AND ONLY TWO POISONOUS SPECIES IN THE WORLD! THOSE WOULD BE THE *GILA MONSTER*, FROM THE WESTERN DESERTS...

"... AND ITS COUSIN, THE *BEADED LIZARD*, FROM MEXICO."

THE ANCIENT SOUTHWEST

OH, HOW MANLY! ANNOYING HELPLESS WILDLIFE!

— YEAH, YOU WISH!

AND WHAT IF IT'S POISONOUS!

HEY!

WANTA SEE SOMETHIN' SCALY?

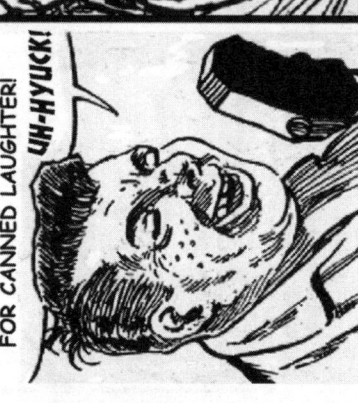

THE ANCIENT SOUTHWEST

BY GEORGE E. TURNER & M.H. PRICE

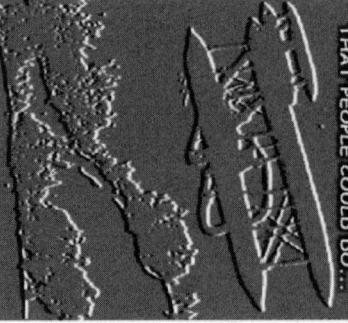

THE ACCOMPLISHMENTS OF HUMANKIND ARE USU- ALLY IMITATIONS OF NATURE. EARLY IN THE LAST CENTURY, FLYING BECAME SOMETHING THAT PEOPLE COULD DO . . .

. . . MILLIONS OF YEARS AFTER THE AGE OF FLYING REPTILES, TO SAY NOTHING OF INSECTS . . .

. . . AND BIRDS, AND EVEN FISH . . .

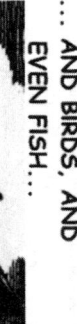

. . . AS WELL AS THE MUCH MORE RECENT FLYING PHALANGER, CAPABLE OF MIGHTY SUR- GES FROM TREE TO TREE.

THE ANCIENT SOUTHWEST

By M.H. Price & George E. Turner

Two sail-backed lizards from prehistoric Texas:

THE CREATURES SHOWN HERE WERE THE FIERCEST OF THEIR TIME — EDAPHOSAURUS (LEFT) AND DIMETRODON. EACH GREW TO A LENGTH OF UP TO 10 FEET. THE PUR- POSE OF THE DORSAL SAIL-LIKE APPARATUS REMAINS A MYSTERY. SCIENCE SUSPECTS IT WAS A HINDRANCE THAT LED TO EXTINCTION. THE SUPPORTS FOR THE RIGID FINS WERE EXTENSIONS OF THE VERTEBRAE.

DIMETRODON WAS THE LARGER AND CRUELER—ARMED WITH VICIOUS INCISORS AS WELL AS TUSKS, THE BETTER TO KILL AND REND ITS PREY.

THE ANCIENT SOUTHWEST

BY M.H. PRICE & GEORGE E. TURNER

The Phytosaur family was a large one, and its members ranged in size up to 20 feet. The nostrils were set in front of the eyes, and were raised so that the beasts could breathe while almost entirely submerged.

Fighting, lashing, crocodile-like Phytosaurs would not have been an unfamiliar sight on the Texas Plains during the Triassic period (over 155 million years ago). Despite the similarity in appearance, the Phytosaurs were not the direct ancestors of today's crocodiles.

The victim shown at right is a Buettneria — a flat-headed amphibian.

THE ANCIENT SOUTHWEST

BY M.H. PRICE & GEORGE E. TURNER

THOUGH TOOTHLESS IN THE FRONT OF ITS MOUTH, THE TRACHODON HAD JAWS CROWDED WITH TINY GRINDERS, AS THESE WORE OUT, MORE LIKE THEM GREW IN!

SO WHO NEEDS A *DENTIST?*

... WHILE THE KNIFE-LIKE TEETH OF THE TYRANNOSAURUS REX BESPEAK A BLOODTHIRSTY APPETITE.

-17-

THE ANCIENT SOUTHWEST

THE WEAK, SMALL TEETH OF THE SAUROPOD DINOSAURS PROVE THAT THESE HUGE CREATURES WERE STRICT VEGETARIANS...

WHILE A WINNING SMILE IS UNDOUBTEDLY OF IMPORTANCE, EVEN TODAY THE CHIEF FUNCTION OF THE TEETH IS TO CHEW.

BY STUDYING FOSSIL TEETH, SCIENTISTS CAN LEARN MUCH.

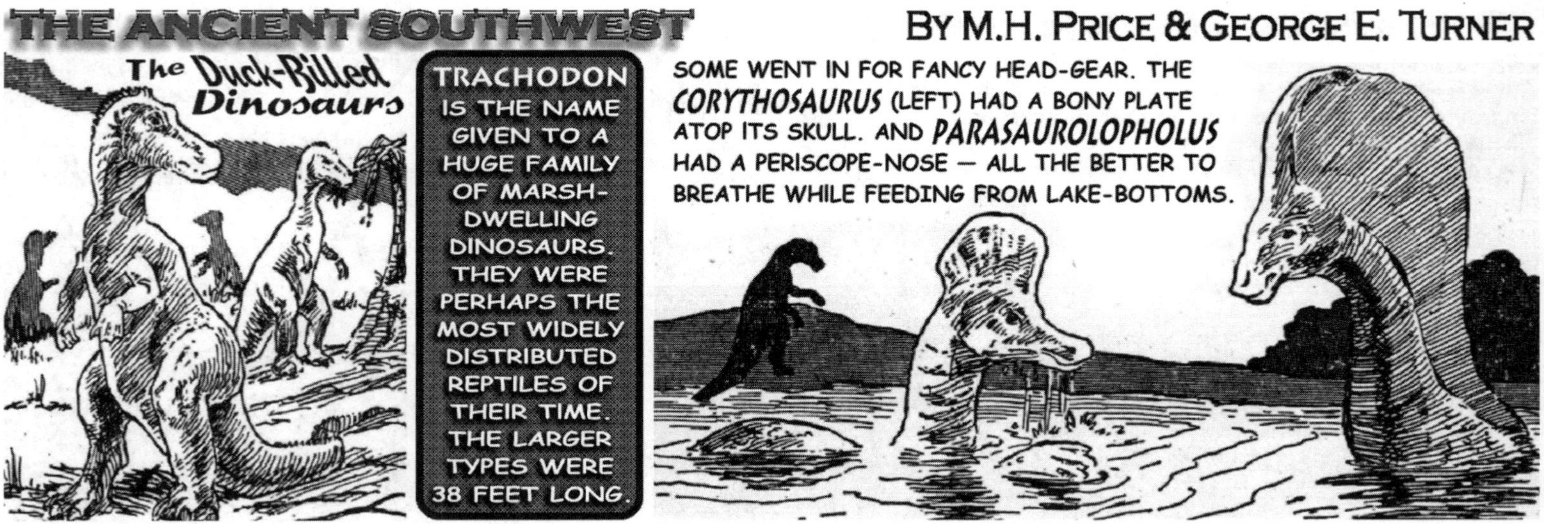
THE ANCIENT SOUTHWEST
BY M.H. PRICE & GEORGE E. TURNER
The Duck-Billed Dinosaurs
TRACHODON IS THE NAME GIVEN TO A HUGE FAMILY OF MARSH-DWELLING DINOSAURS. THEY WERE PERHAPS THE MOST WIDELY DISTRIBUTED REPTILES OF THEIR TIME. THE LARGER TYPES WERE 38 FEET LONG.
SOME WENT IN FOR FANCY HEAD-GEAR. THE CORYTHOSAURUS (LEFT) HAD A BONY PLATE ATOP ITS SKULL. AND PARASAUROLOPHOLUS HAD A PERISCOPE-NOSE — ALL THE BETTER TO BREATHE WHILE FEEDING FROM LAKE-BOTTOMS.

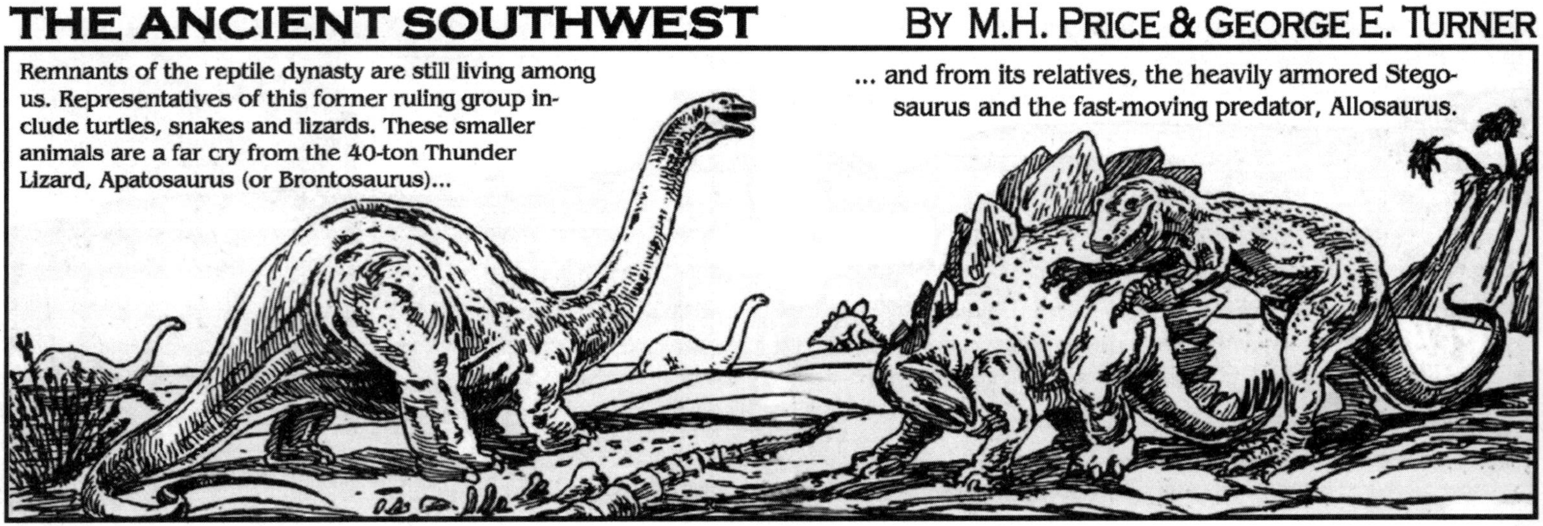
THE ANCIENT SOUTHWEST
BY M.H. PRICE & GEORGE E. TURNER
Remnants of the reptile dynasty are still living among us. Representatives of this former ruling group include turtles, snakes and lizards. These smaller animals are a far cry from the 40-ton Thunder Lizard, Apatosaurus (or Brontosaurus)...
... and from its relatives, the heavily armored Stegosaurus and the fast-moving predator, Allosaurus.

THE ANCIENT SOUTHWEST

BY M.H. PRICE & GEORGE E. TURNER

MANY PEOPLE HAVE REPORTED SEEING THE FABLED *LOCH NESS MONSTER*, BUT NO ONE HAS PRODUCED ANY PROOF.

YET IN THE ANCIENT SEAS THAT SURGED FROM TEXAS INTO KANSAS SEA SERPENTS FLOURISHED. THESE **PLESIOSAURS** GREW TO FIFTY FEET IN LENGTH.

THEIR MOST DANGEROUS WEAPON WAS A LONG AND FLEXIBLE NECK, WHICH COULD BE THRUST IN ANY DIRECTION.

THE ANCIENT SOUTHWEST

BY M.H. PRICE & GEORGE E. TURNER

MUCH MORE UNUSUAL WERE THE MARINE CROCS OF THE JURASSIC ERA. THESE CREATURES TOOK TO THE SEAS SO WELL THAT THEY APPARENTLY LOST THEIR ARMOR, REDEVELOPED THEIR TAILS FOR SWIMMING AND DEVELOPED PADDLES IN PLACE OF FEET.

IN THE COURSE OF MILLIONS OF YEARS, THE *CROCODILE* FAMILY HAS CHANGED BUT VERY LITTLE.

THERE HAVE BEEN SOME UNUSUAL SPECIMENS, EVEN SO.

THIS PARTICULAR TYPE LIVED IN COLORADO ABOUT 50 MILLION YEARS AGO. IT SPORTED HORNS AND WAS OVERALL WELL ARMORED.

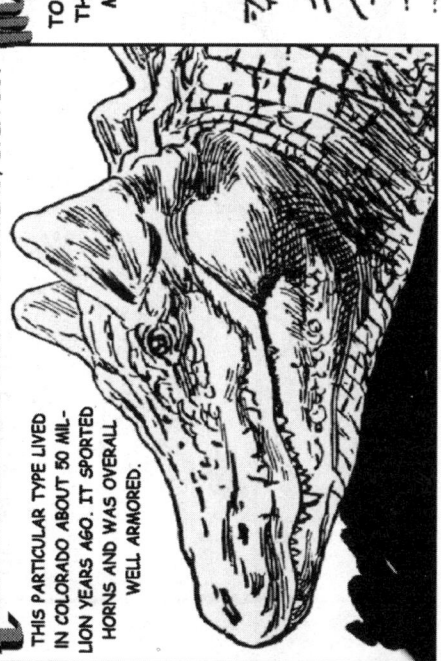

THE ANCIENT SOUTHWEST

By M.H. Price & George E. Turner

THERE HAVE BEEN SOME BIG ONES, HOWEVER — SUCH AS THE CREATURE SHOWN BELOW. LARGE AND FIERCE, IT WAS — AND NO DOUBT A MATCH FOR ANY OTHER BEAST.

40 FEET LONG? WHAT A CROC'!

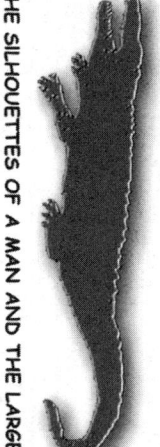

THE SILHOUETTES OF A MAN AND THE LARGEST TYPE OF MODERN-DAY CROCODILE (ABOVE) ARE DRAWN TO SCALE FOR COMPARISON WITH THE 40-FOOT-LONG MONSTER SHOWN BELOW...

MOST OF THE EARLY KNOWN CROCODILES WERE DWARFED REPTILES, TWO OR THREE FEET IN LENGTH.

-20-

THE ANCIENT SOUTHWEST

By M.H. Price & George E. Turner

AMONG THE MORE BIZARRE DEVELOPMENTS OF THE AGE OF REPTILES WERE THE SO-CALLED FLYING LIZARDS — *PTERODACTYLS.*

MOST OF THE WINGED REPTILES WERE SMALL....

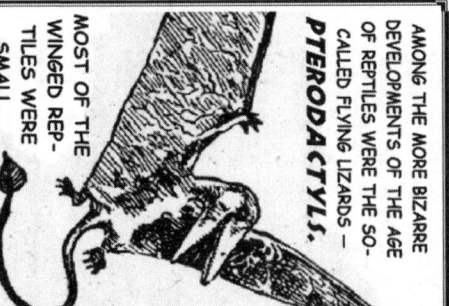

... BUT THE MOST SPEC-TACULAR GROUP, CALLED PTERANODONS...

... HAD A WINGSPREAD OF NEARLY 30 FEET.

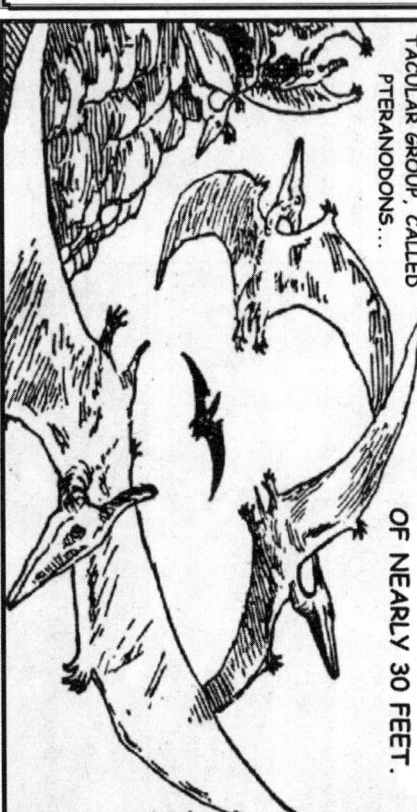

PTERODACTYL MEANS "WING-FINGER"...

... IN THAT THE ENTIRE WING WAS SUPPORTED BY AN ELON-GATED DIGIT.

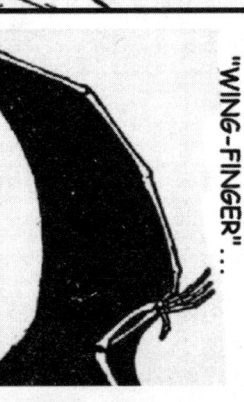

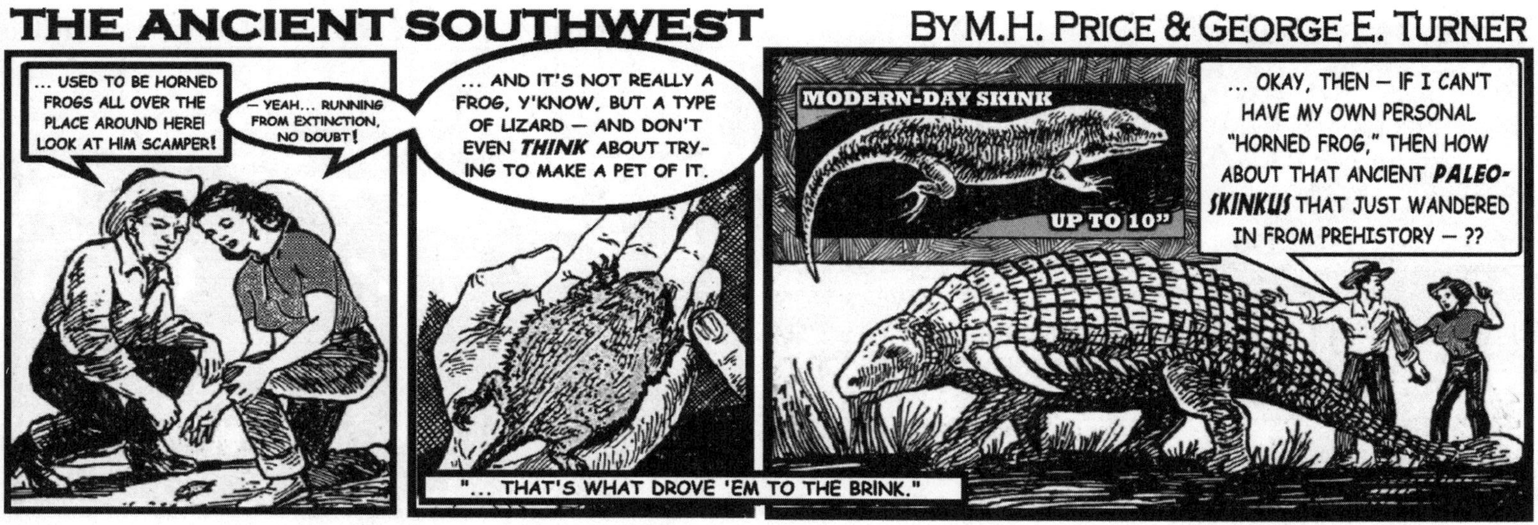
THE ANCIENT SOUTHWEST
BY M.H. PRICE & GEORGE E. TURNER
... USED TO BE HORNED FROGS ALL OVER THE PLACE AROUND HERE! LOOK AT HIM SCAMPER!
— YEAH... RUNNING FROM EXTINCTION, NO DOUBT!
... AND IT'S NOT REALLY A FROG, Y'KNOW, BUT A TYPE OF LIZARD — AND DON'T EVEN THINK ABOUT TRYING TO MAKE A PET OF IT.
MODERN-DAY SKINK
UP TO 10"
... OKAY, THEN — IF I CAN'T HAVE MY OWN PERSONAL "HORNED FROG," THEN HOW ABOUT THAT ANCIENT PALEO-SKINKUS THAT JUST WANDERED IN FROM PREHISTORY — ??
"... THAT'S WHAT DROVE 'EM TO THE BRINK."

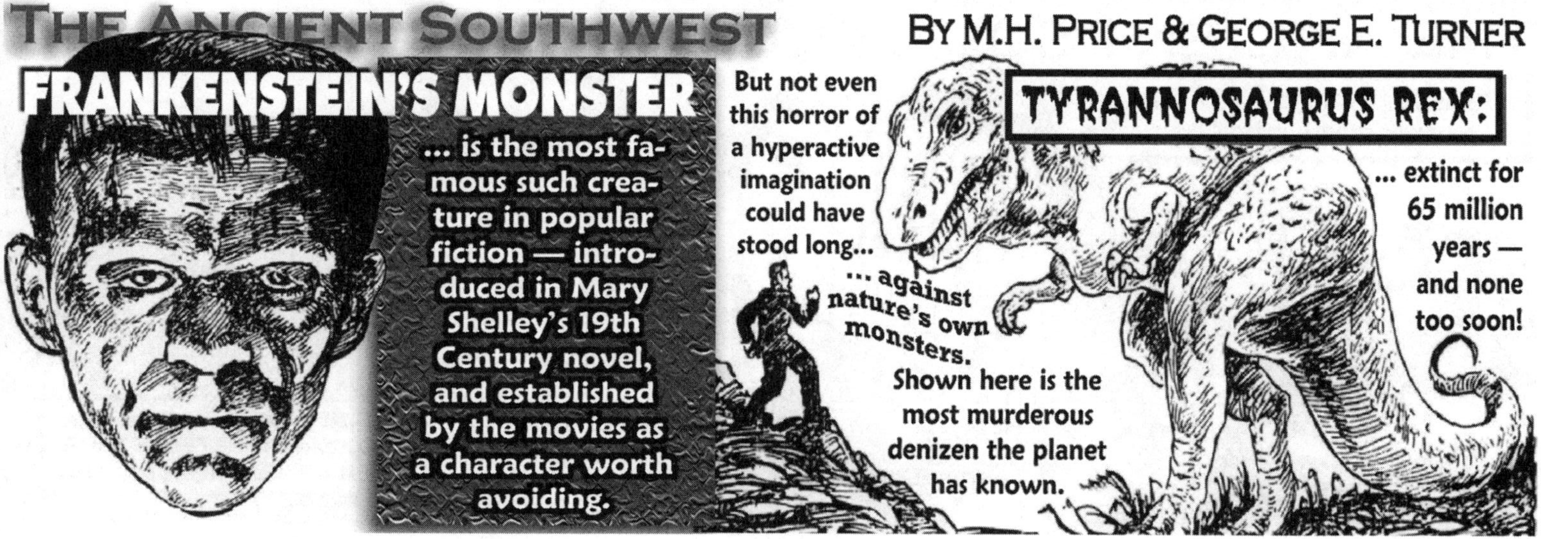
THE ANCIENT SOUTHWEST
BY M.H. PRICE & GEORGE E. TURNER
FRANKENSTEIN'S MONSTER
... is the most famous such creature in popular fiction — introduced in Mary Shelley's 19th Century novel, and established by the movies as a character worth avoiding.
But not even this horror of a hyperactive imagination could have stood long...
... against nature's own monsters.
TYRANNOSAURUS REX:
... extinct for 65 million years — and none too soon!
Shown here is the most murderous denizen the planet has known.

THE ANCIENT SOUTHWEST

KING KONG LIVES!

By M.H. Price & George E. Turner

THE CHRONIC POPULARITY OF THIS MOST FAMOUS OF ALL GIANT-APE THRILLERS OFTEN LEAVES VIEWERS WONDERING ABOUT THE SUPPOSED ACCURACY OF THE FILM'S CELEBRATED PREHISTORIC CREATURE SCENES.

(NO DOUBT WHETHER KONG HIMSELF IS IMAGINARY—RIGHT?)

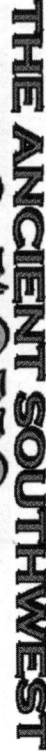

AS SEEN IN "KING KONG" ...

FROM LEFT: STEGOSAURUS; DESMATOSUCHUS; PLESIOSAURUS; PTERANODON

LEFT: TYRANNOSAURUS; ABOVE: APATOSAURUS, A.K.A. BRONTOSAURUS.

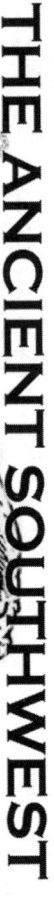

THE ANCIENT SOUTHWEST

By Price & Turner

IT SEEMS UNLIKELY THAT THE HUGE QUADRUPEDAL DINOSAURS SPENT MUCH TIME ON DRY LAND.

THEY PROBABLY SPENT MOST OF THEIR TIME IN THE WATER, WHICH HELPED TO SUPPORT THEIR BULK.

NOT TO MENTION THAT THEIR LACK OF ARMOR AND THEIR FEEBLE TEETH LEFT THEM HELPLESS WHEN AGROUND.

THE ANCIENT SOUTHWEST

By M.H. Price & George E. Turner

GIVE THIS MEEK LIT-TLE BIRD A LOOK AT ITS FAMILY ALBUM...

... AND IT MIGHT SNAP THE TAIL OFF THE OLD TOMCAT.

FOR THE BIRDS ARE DESCENDED FROM THOSE FEARSOME BEASTS OF OLD — THE DINOSAURS.

THE EARLY BIRDS SHARED THE SKIES WITH FLYING LIZARDS — WHICH WERE MORE A TANGENT THAN A STAGE OF AVIAN DEVELOPMENT.

THE ANCIENT SOUTHWEST

By M.H. Price & George E. Turner

... OR SMILODON'S REGAL CONTEMPORARY, THE FELIS ATROX — WHICH STOOD ABOUT ONE-QUARTER LARGER THAN THE MIGHTY AFRICAN LION OF THE PRESENT DAY.

CATS!

... SUCH AS THE GREAT SABRE-TOOTH, SMILO-DON — WHICH WAS MORE FORMIDABLE THAN EVEN THE BIGGER CATS OF TODAY, WITH TUSKS A FOOT IN LENGTH...

IT'S TEMPTING TO WONDER WHAT OUR MODERN-DAY FELINES MIGHT THINK OF THEIR MOST DISTANT ANCESTORS...

THE ANCIENT SOUTHWEST

By M.H. Price & George E. Turner

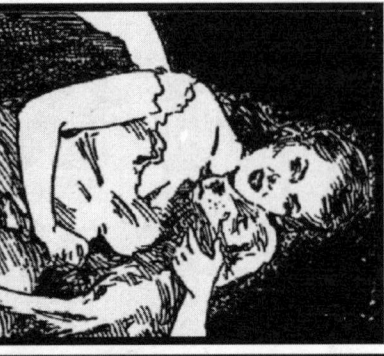

DOGS BEFORE DOMESTICATION WERE HARDLY THE TYPE TO COM-MANDEER A COZY LAP.

NO, THEY WERE MORE THE SORT TO INSPIRE TERROR. THE SIZE OF ONE SUCH MONSTER, THE DINOCYON, MAY BE CALCULATED BY THE COMPARATIVE STATURE OF THE COCKER SPANIEL SHOWN IN THE CENTER.

A PACK OF THESE BEASTS, HUNTING ON THE TEXAS PRAIRIES, MUST HAVE BEEN AN AWE-SOME SIGHT!

THE ANCIENT SOUTHWEST
Sea of MONSTERS!

By M.H. Price & George E. Turner

THE OCEAN THAT COVERED TEXAS, KANSAS AND OKLAHOMA DURING CRE-TACEOUS TIMES WAS THE HOME OF SUCH TERRORS AS THESE:

THE TWENTY-FOOT EATING MACHINE KNOWN AS *PORTHEUS*

ARCHELON: A 12-FOOT TURTLE

THIS SWIMMING LIZARD WAS INDEED A MONSTER OF THE SEAS, FEROCIOUS AND WELL-ARMED. SOME GREW TO FIFTY FEET IN LENGTH.

MOSOSAURUS

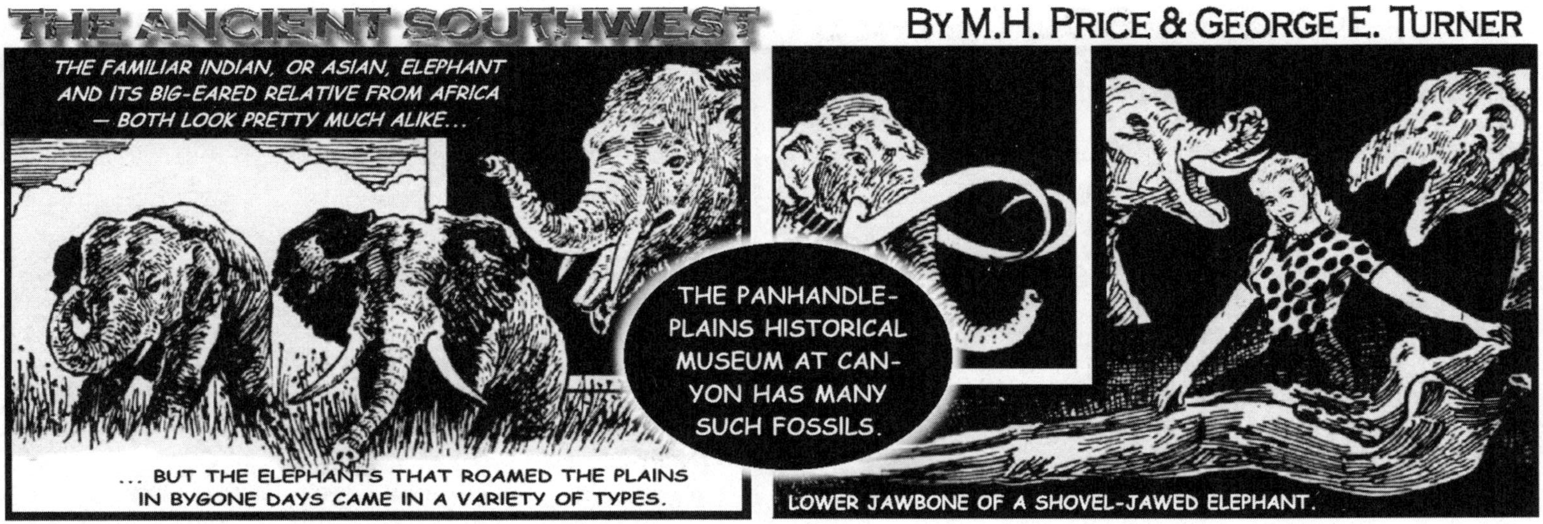
THE ANCIENT SOUTHWEST
BY M.H. PRICE & GEORGE E. TURNER
THE FAMILIAR INDIAN, OR ASIAN, ELEPHANT AND ITS BIG-EARED RELATIVE FROM AFRICA — BOTH LOOK PRETTY MUCH ALIKE...
... BUT THE ELEPHANTS THAT ROAMED THE PLAINS IN BYGONE DAYS CAME IN A VARIETY OF TYPES.
THE PANHANDLE-PLAINS HISTORICAL MUSEUM AT CANYON HAS MANY SUCH FOSSILS.
LOWER JAWBONE OF A SHOVEL-JAWED ELEPHANT.

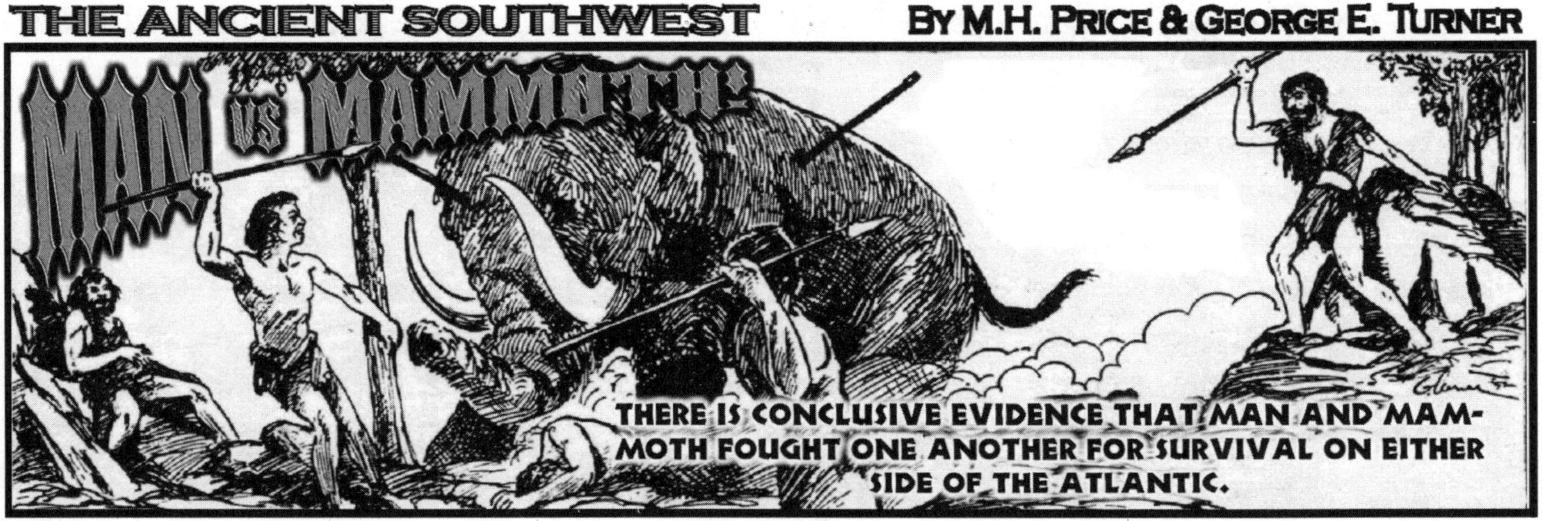
THE ANCIENT SOUTHWEST
BY M.H. PRICE & GEORGE E. TURNER
MAN VS MAMMOTH!
THERE IS CONCLUSIVE EVIDENCE THAT MAN AND MAMMOTH FOUGHT ONE ANOTHER FOR SURVIVAL ON EITHER SIDE OF THE ATLANTIC.

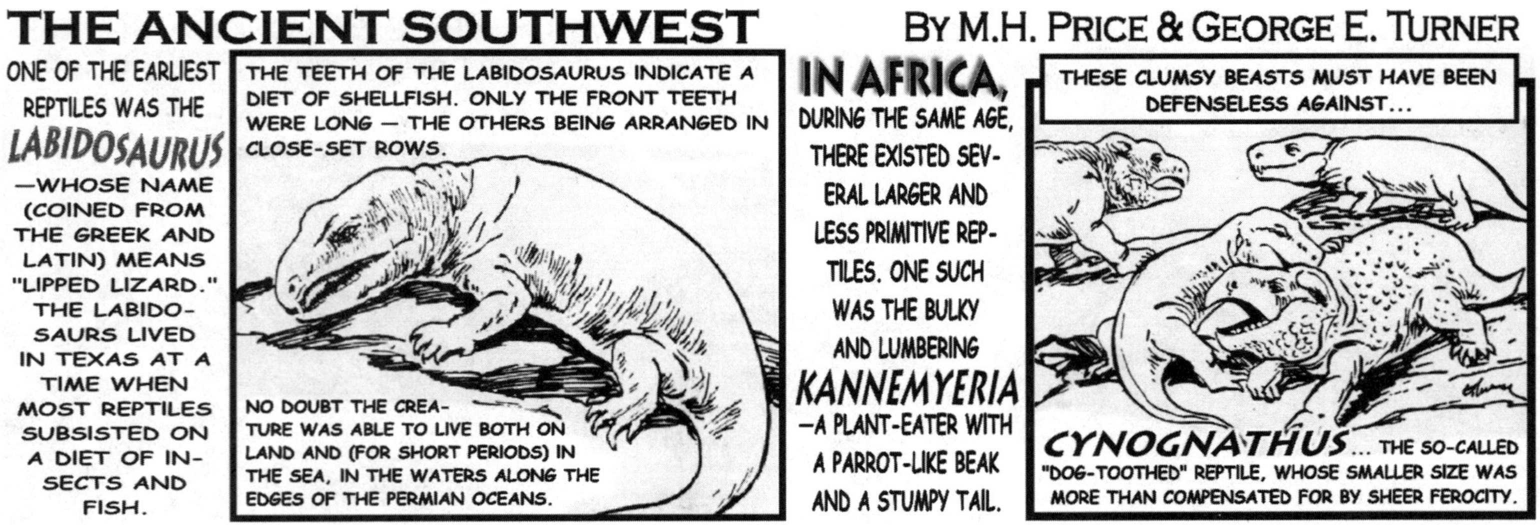
THE ANCIENT SOUTHWEST
BY M.H. PRICE & GEORGE E. TURNER
ONE OF THE EARLIEST REPTILES WAS THE LABIDOSAURUS —WHOSE NAME (COINED FROM THE GREEK AND LATIN) MEANS "LIPPED LIZARD." THE LABIDOSAURS LIVED IN TEXAS AT A TIME WHEN MOST REPTILES SUBSISTED ON A DIET OF INSECTS AND FISH.
THE TEETH OF THE LABIDOSAURUS INDICATE A DIET OF SHELLFISH. ONLY THE FRONT TEETH WERE LONG — THE OTHERS BEING ARRANGED IN CLOSE-SET ROWS.
NO DOUBT THE CREATURE WAS ABLE TO LIVE BOTH ON LAND AND (FOR SHORT PERIODS) IN THE SEA, IN THE WATERS ALONG THE EDGES OF THE PERMIAN OCEANS.
IN AFRICA, DURING THE SAME AGE, THERE EXISTED SEVERAL LARGER AND LESS PRIMITIVE REPTILES. ONE SUCH WAS THE BULKY AND LUMBERING KANNEMYERIA —A PLANT-EATER WITH A PARROT-LIKE BEAK AND A STUMPY TAIL.
THESE CLUMSY BEASTS MUST HAVE BEEN DEFENSELESS AGAINST...
CYNOGNATHUS... THE SO-CALLED "DOG-TOOTHED" REPTILE, WHOSE SMALLER SIZE WAS MORE THAN COMPENSATED FOR BY SHEER FEROCITY.

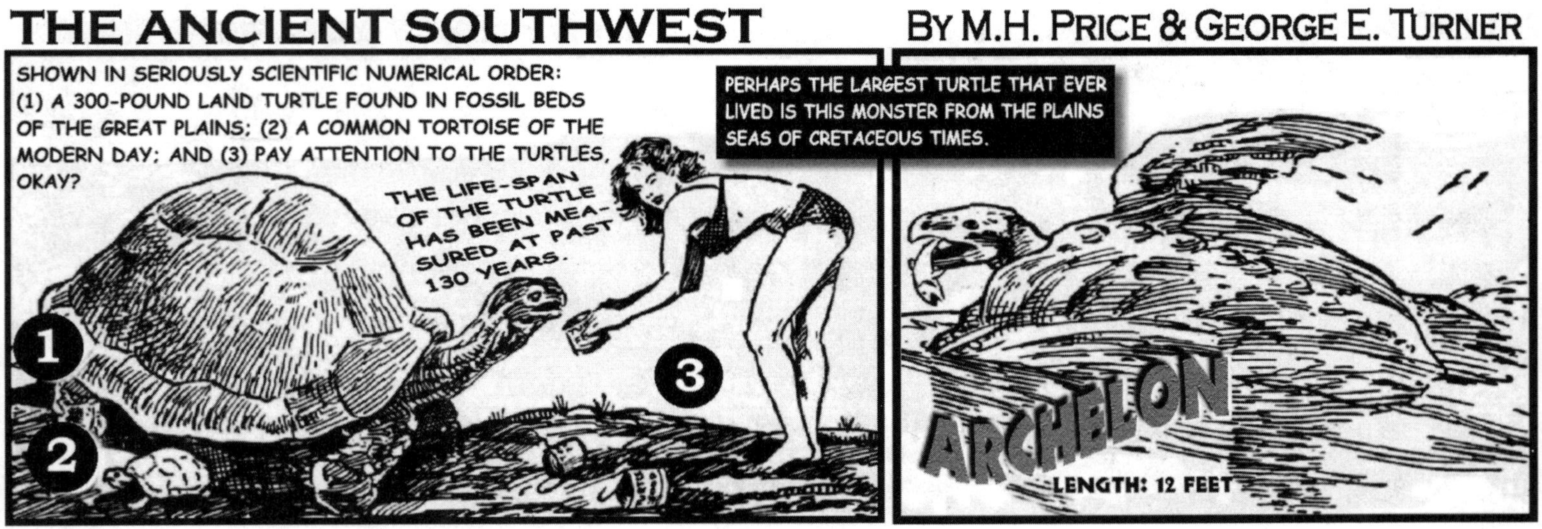
THE ANCIENT SOUTHWEST
BY M.H. PRICE & GEORGE E. TURNER
SHOWN IN SERIOUSLY SCIENTIFIC NUMERICAL ORDER: (1) A 300-POUND LAND TURTLE FOUND IN FOSSIL BEDS OF THE GREAT PLAINS; (2) A COMMON TORTOISE OF THE MODERN DAY; AND (3) PAY ATTENTION TO THE TURTLES, OKAY?
THE LIFE-SPAN OF THE TURTLE HAS BEEN MEASURED AT PAST 130 YEARS.
1
2
3
PERHAPS THE LARGEST TURTLE THAT EVER LIVED IS THIS MONSTER FROM THE PLAINS SEAS OF CRETACEOUS TIMES.
ARCHELON
LENGTH: 12 FEET

THE ANCIENT SOUTHWEST

By M.H. PRICE & GEORGE E. TURNER

— SPEAKING OF UNUSUAL ANIMALS, THAT ONE JUST ABOUT TAKES THE CAKE! WE CALL HIM *MOROPUS* — A REAL RARITY!

WHAT ON EARTH DID HE LOOK LIKE ALIVE?

"LIKE NOTHING ON EARTH TODAY, THAT'S FOR SURE! A LITTLE BIT LIKE A HORSE, ONLY BIGGER, WITH CLAWS ON ALL FOUR FEET!"

Moropus Elatus
(Lower Miocene, U.S.)

THE PURPOSE OF THE CLAWS IS STILL A PUZZLER.

— PROBABLY TO REMIND YOU THAT YOU NEED A MANICURE!

THE ANCIENT SOUTHWEST

By M.H. PRICE & GEORGE E. TURNER

If Plains hunters could go back a few tens of millions of years, they would see...

... a strange, deer-like animal with forkéd horns on its snout... herds of gigantic, giraffe-like camels...

... and humongous wild pigs!

THE ANCIENT SOUTHWEST

By M.H. Price & George E. Turner

By M.H. Price & George E. Turner

A reader inquires: "Was the dinosaur the biggest animal ever?"

ANSWER: NO.

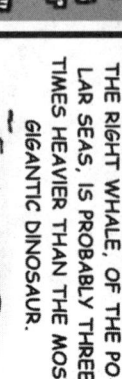

THE RIGHT WHALE, OF THE POLAR SEAS, IS PROBABLY THREE TIMES HEAVIER THAN THE MOST GIGANTIC DINOSAUR.

RIGHT!

50 TONS OF DINOSAUR

— THAT'S THE ESTIMATED WEIGHT OF THE CREATURE WHOSE FORE-LEG BONE IS SHOWN HERE.

6 ft.

THIS SPECIMEN, CALLED BRACHIOSAURUS, IS BELIEVED TO HAVE BEEN THE LARGEST OF LAND ANIMALS.

THE LONGEST KNOWN DINOSAUR IS THE 87-FOOTER — DIPLODOCUS.

DWARVES AMONG GIANTS

MOST OF US THINK OF THE DINOSAURS AS A RACE OF GIANTS, BUT AMONG THE MORE THAN 5,000 SPECIES ARE SEVERAL WHOSE TININESS SEEMS INCREDIBLE IN VIEW OF THE IMMENSITY OF SOME.

THE TREE-DWELLER *HYPSILOPHODON* WAS ABOUT A YARD IN LENGTH AND THRIVED DURING THE LAST PERIOD OF REPTILIAN SUPREMACY.

PODOKESAURUS WAS A FLESH-EATER OF THE LATE TRIASSIC PERIOD — MORE FEROCIOUS AND BLOODTHISTY THAN MOST OF THE LARGER REPTILES...

... DESPITE ITS THREE-FOOT LENGTH.

CAMPSOGNATHUS

MANY SUCH DINOSAURS WERE NO LARGER THAN RABBITS OR CHICKENS.

THE ANCIENT SOUTHWEST

By M.H. Price & George E. Turner

THE LONG-HORNED BISON WAS ABOUT TWICE THE SIZE OF A MO-DERN-DAY BISON (a.k.a. BUFFALO). THE INSIDE CURVE OF ITS HORNS MEASURED ABOUT TEN FEET.

ONE DOUBTS THAT ANY FIGHTER OF BULLS WOULD CARE TO ENTER THE RING WITH THIS NOW-EX-TINCT DENI-ZEN OF THE TEXAS PLAINS.

ARMED WITH ONLY A SWORD AND AIDED BY ONLY A CREW OF FOUR, A HERO OF THE A-RENA EARNS THE APPROVAL OF A CHEERING CROWD...

... BY BRAVELY KILLING A DOMESTICATED BULL.

THE ANCIENT SOUTHWEST

By M.H. Price & George E. Turner

... THUS RENDERING THE MIGHTY CREA-TURES EASY PREY FOR PRIMITIVE WEAPONS.

WAS BUFFALO HUNTING EVER A SPORTING PRO-POSITION?

CERTAINLY NOT IN THE DAY OF THE PALEO-INDIANS, WHO WOULD STAMPEDE THE HERDS OVER CAN-YON WALLS...

THE ANCIENT SOUTHWEST

The March of Civilization

By M.H. Price & George E. Turner

The dinosaurs were a savage and vicious group, often staging vicious battles in order to live. Humankind is of course superior to such beasts. This superiority, in turn, has brought about means of destruction far more effective than any means at the disposal of a T-Rex.

YES, AND HOW TIMES HAVE CHANGED!

BOOM!

THE ANCIENT SOUTHWEST

By M.H. Price & George E. Turner

The operative term is "legendary."

The Unicorn is a legendary animal with a single horn on its forehead.

But there sure enough was a....

TYRANOSAURUS

THIS 25-FOOTER WAS A (COMPARATIVELY) HARMLESS VEGETARIAN.

THE ANCIENT SOUTHWEST

By M.H. Price & George E. Turner

A living one-horned creature is the male narwhal, whose left front tooth forms a horn-like tusk.

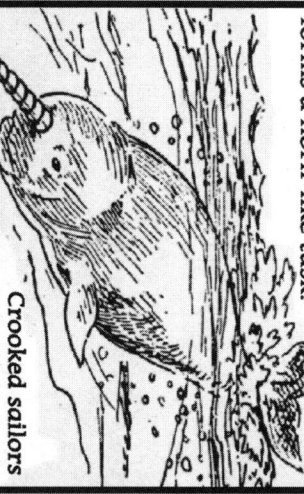

Crooked sailors often sell these tusks — passing them off as Unicorn horns.

THE ANCIENT SOUTHWEST

By M.H. Price & George E. Turner

THROUGHOUT THE AGES, THE PEACE-LOVERS OF THE WORLD HAVE DEALT WITH AGGRESSORS.

AGE OF REPTILES: STEGOSAURUS TURNS THE TABLES ON A FLESH-EATER.

AGE OF MAMMALS: THE ARMADILLO-LIKE GLYPTODON USES ITS SPIKED TAIL TO DISABLE A SABRE-TOOTH.

MODERN TIMES: THE COYOTE CAN SAVE ITSELF SOME GRIEF MERELY BY ALLOWING THE SKUNK TO PASS UNDISTURBED.

THE ANCIENT SOUTHWEST

By M.H. Price & George E. Turner

250 YEARS AGO, IN NEW ENGLAND:

WHY, WE'VE UNEARTHED THE GRAVE OF SOME *OGRE!*

HE MUST HAVE BEEN EIGHTY FEET TALL!

— AND HERE'S ONE OF HIS TEETH — IT WEIGHS NEARLY *FIVE POUNDS!*

A PHYSICIAN FOUND THE BONES TO HAVE COME FROM AN ELEPHANT.

AMATEURS!

IT TURNED OUT TO BE A PREHISTORIC ELEPHANT KNOWN AS A *MASTODON!* HOW ABOUT THAT?

AND NOT JUST ANY ELEPHANT, AT THAT.

THE ANCIENT SOUTHWEST

BY M.H. PRICE & GEORGE E. TURNER

DEVOTEES OF THE HORSE ARE ALWAYS FASCINATED TO LOOK BACK AT A LONG AND COMPLICATED LINEAGE....

... TO THE OLIGOCENE AGE, FOR EX-AMPLE, WHEN A SMALL, THREE-TOED HORSE RANGED AT LARGE...

Uhm – DID SOMEBODY SAY "LARGE" – ?

THIS BRUISER WOULD BE A *BRONTOTHERE* – A MORE DISTANT ANCES-TOR OF THE HORSE.

THE ANCIENT SOUTHWEST

BY M.H. PRICE & GEORGE E. TURNER

MEGATHERIUM

MEANS "GREAT BEAST." THIS GIANT GROUND SLOTH STOOD 16 FEET TALL. HE LIVED IN THE SOUTHWESTERN U.S. AND SOUTH AMERICA DURING THE **ICE AGE.**

A harmless vegetarian, the Mega-therium is known to have provided easy prey for primitive humankind.

A LIVING DESCENDANT IS THE SMALL, TREE-DWELLING SLOTH OF SOUTH A-MERICA, WHICH HABITUALLY HANGS UPSIDE-DOWN FROM HIGH LIMBS.

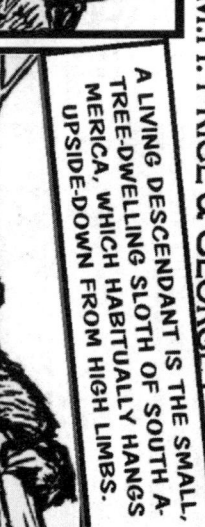

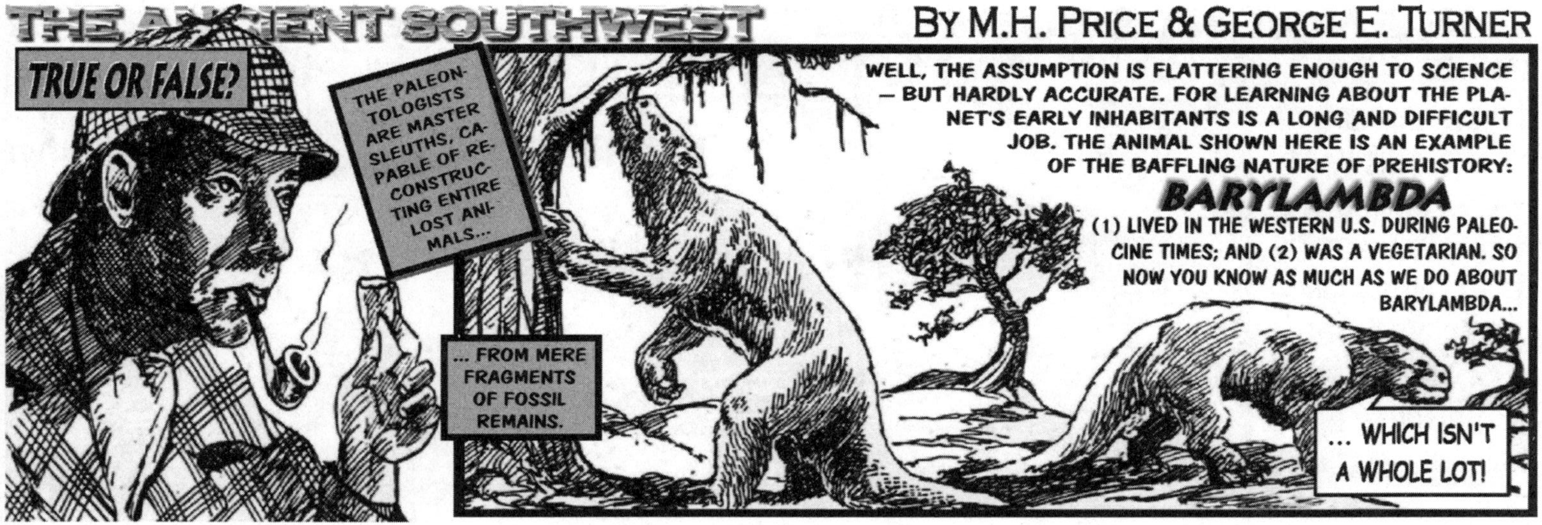
THE ANCIENT SOUTHWEST
BY M.H. PRICE & GEORGE E. TURNER
TRUE OR FALSE?
THE PALEONTOLOGISTS ARE MASTER SLEUTHS, CAPABLE OF RECONSTRUCTING ENTIRE LOST ANIMALS...
... FROM MERE FRAGMENTS OF FOSSIL REMAINS.
WELL, THE ASSUMPTION IS FLATTERING ENOUGH TO SCIENCE — BUT HARDLY ACCURATE. FOR LEARNING ABOUT THE PLANET'S EARLY INHABITANTS IS A LONG AND DIFFICULT JOB. THE ANIMAL SHOWN HERE IS AN EXAMPLE OF THE BAFFLING NATURE OF PREHISTORY:
BARYLAMBDA
(1) LIVED IN THE WESTERN U.S. DURING PALEOCINE TIMES; AND (2) WAS A VEGETARIAN. SO NOW YOU KNOW AS MUCH AS WE DO ABOUT BARYLAMBDA...
... WHICH ISN'T A WHOLE LOT!

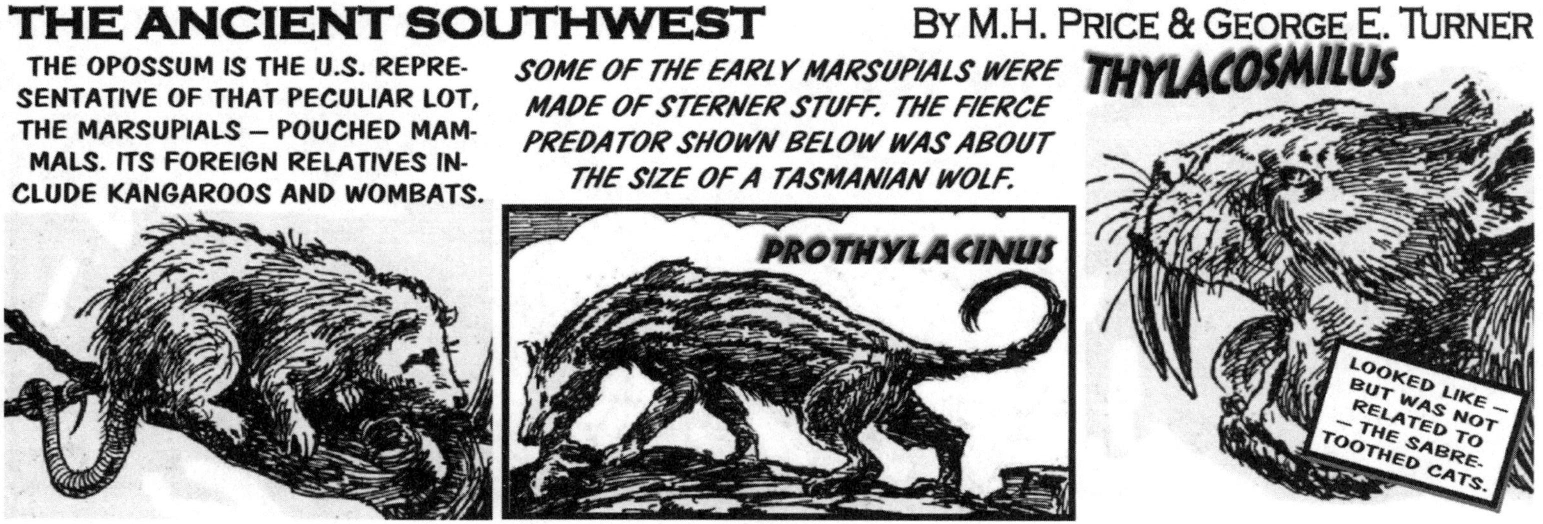
THE ANCIENT SOUTHWEST
BY M.H. PRICE & GEORGE E. TURNER
THE OPOSSUM IS THE U.S. REPRESENTATIVE OF THAT PECULIAR LOT, THE MARSUPIALS — POUCHED MAMMALS. ITS FOREIGN RELATIVES INCLUDE KANGAROOS AND WOMBATS.
SOME OF THE EARLY MARSUPIALS WERE MADE OF STERNER STUFF. THE FIERCE PREDATOR SHOWN BELOW WAS ABOUT THE SIZE OF A TASMANIAN WOLF.
PROTHYLACINUS
THYLACOSMILUS
LOOKED LIKE — BUT WAS NOT RELATED TO — THE SABRE-TOOTHED CATS.

THE ANCIENT SOUTHWEST

By M.H. Price & George E. Turner

PEMMICAN! EASY TO FIX! SIMPLE TO SERVE! DEE-LICIOUS!

PEMMICAN — AT HOME!

FOR HUNDREDS OF YEARS, THIS TASTY DISH FORMED THE PRINCIPAL DIET OF THE PLAINS INDIAN! NOW, YOU, TOO, CAN ENJOY THE DELIGHTS OF *PEMMICAN* — AT HOME!

GRIND SUN-DRIED MEAT TOGETHER WITH PLENTY OF FAT AND BERRIES...

WRAP MIXTURE IN SKINS AND BURY IN BACKYARD UNTIL RIPENED.

NEIGHBOR, HOW LONG HAS IT BEEN?

IGNORE THE PUNGENT AROMA, AND YOU'RE IN FOR SOME MIGHTY FINE EATIN'!

THE ANCIENT SOUTHWEST

EARLY FARMING IN TEXAS

By M.H. Price & George E. Turner

THE EARLIEST TEXANS DID NOT LIVE IN THE CITIFIED SET-TLEMENTS WE KNOW TODAY, BUT IN VILLA-GES ALONG THE RIVERS, WHERE THEY GREW WHAT CROPS THE LAND WOULD SUPPORT.

ANOTHER LIVELIHOOD LAY IN HUNTING. IN MANY RESPECTS, THEIR LIVES WERE NOT MUCH DIFFERENT FROM THOSE OF RURAL FOLKS NOWADAYS.

WE OWE THIS KNOWLEDGE TO THE RELENTLESS INTEREST OF SCIENTISTS — BOTH PRO-FESSIONALS AND AMATEURS.

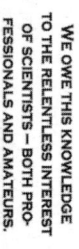

THE ANCIENT SOUTHWEST

BY M.H. PRICE & GEORGE E. TURNER

The Original Bonehead: *UINTATHERIUM*

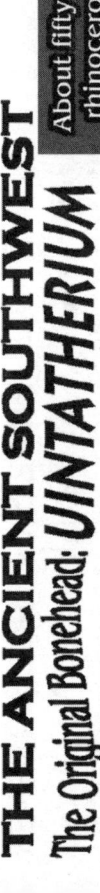

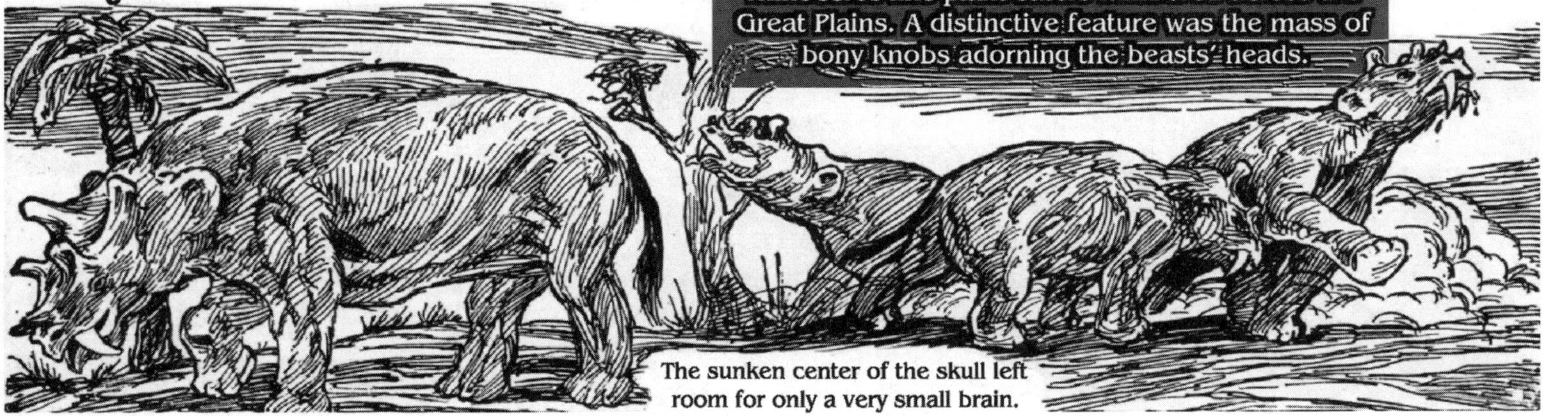
About fifty million years ago, herds of these weird, rhinoceros-like plant-eaters lumbered across the Great Plains. A distinctive feature was the mass of bony knobs adorning the beasts' heads.

The sunken center of the skull left room for only a very small brain.

THE ANCIENT SOUTHWEST

BY M.H. PRICE & GEORGE E. TURNER

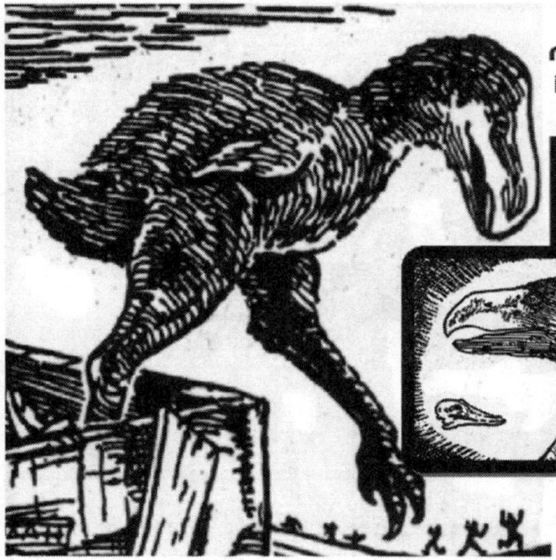

Gigantic prehistoric birds? Look no farther than Texas. One of ours is the Diatryma, shown (inset) for scale with the skull of an ostrich.

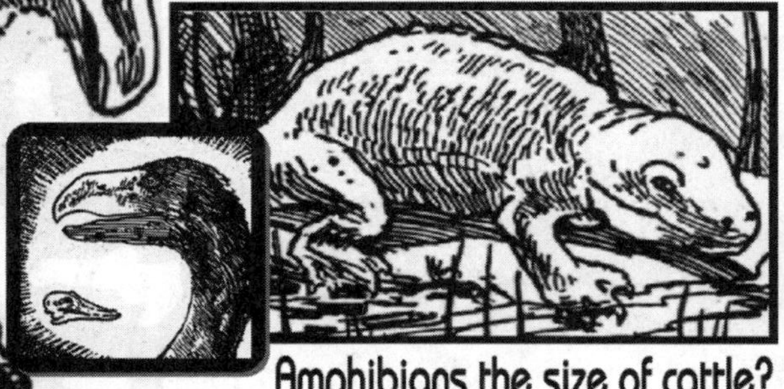

Amphibians the size of cattle?

They come with the territory around these parts.

And don't forget the SHARKTOPUS

Terror of the Gulf!

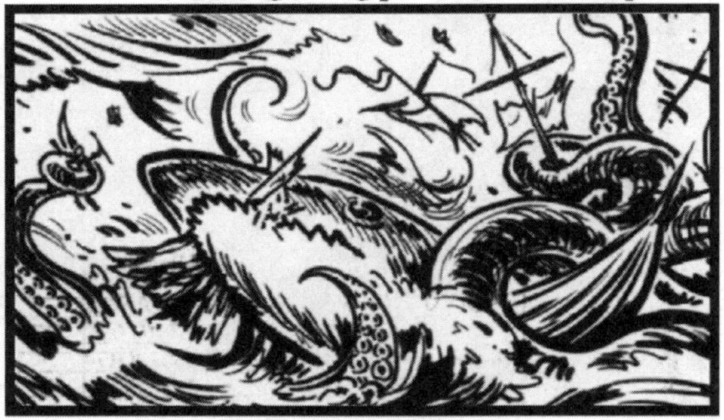

Just kidding about the Sharktopus.
But not about the others.

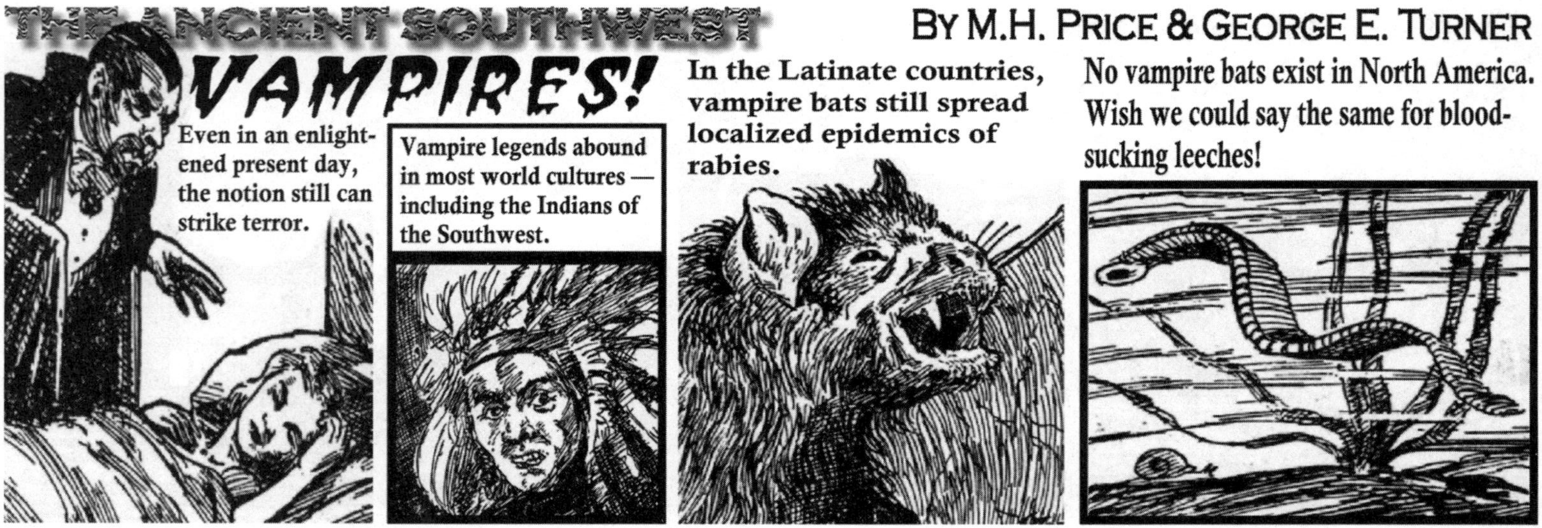
THE ANCIENT SOUTHWEST
BY M.H. PRICE & GEORGE E. TURNER
VAMPIRES!
Even in an enlightened present day, the notion still can strike terror.
Vampire legends abound in most world cultures — including the Indians of the Southwest.
In the Latinate countries, vampire bats still spread localized epidemics of rabies.
No vampire bats exist in North America. Wish we could say the same for blood-sucking leeches!

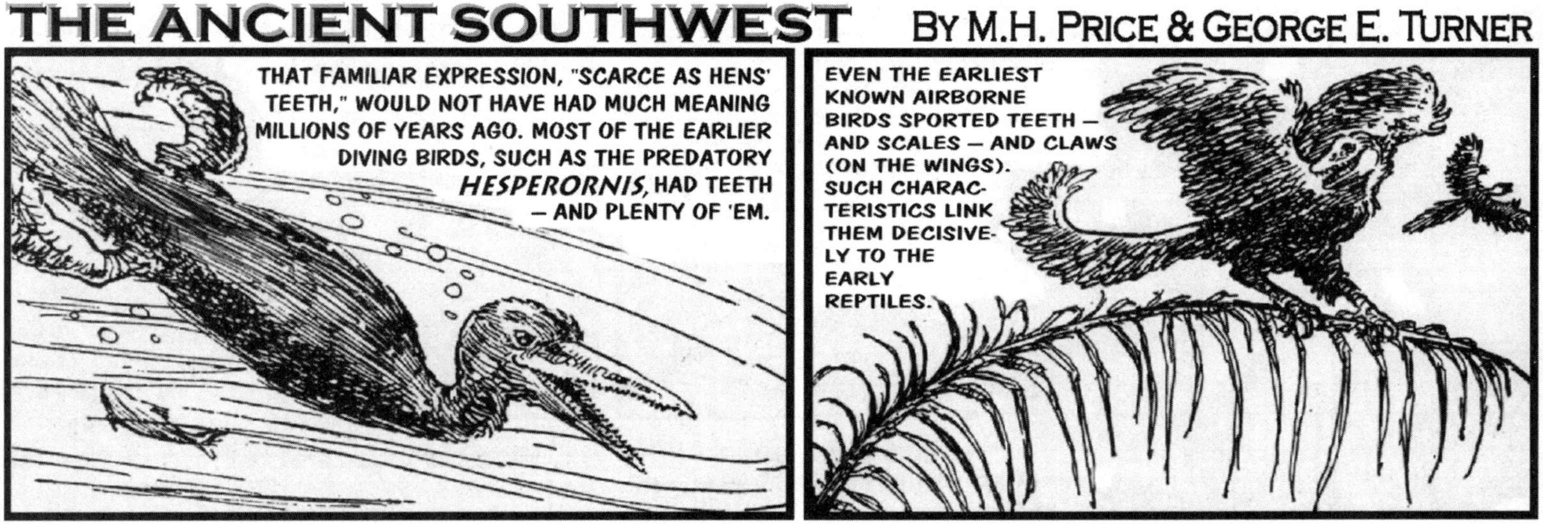
THE ANCIENT SOUTHWEST
BY M.H. PRICE & GEORGE E. TURNER
THAT FAMILIAR EXPRESSION, "SCARCE AS HENS' TEETH," WOULD NOT HAVE HAD MUCH MEANING MILLIONS OF YEARS AGO. MOST OF THE EARLIER DIVING BIRDS, SUCH AS THE PREDATORY HESPERORNIS, HAD TEETH — AND PLENTY OF 'EM.
EVEN THE EARLIEST KNOWN AIRBORNE BIRDS SPORTED TEETH — AND SCALES — AND CLAWS (ON THE WINGS). SUCH CHARACTERISTICS LINK THEM DECISIVELY TO THE EARLY REPTILES.

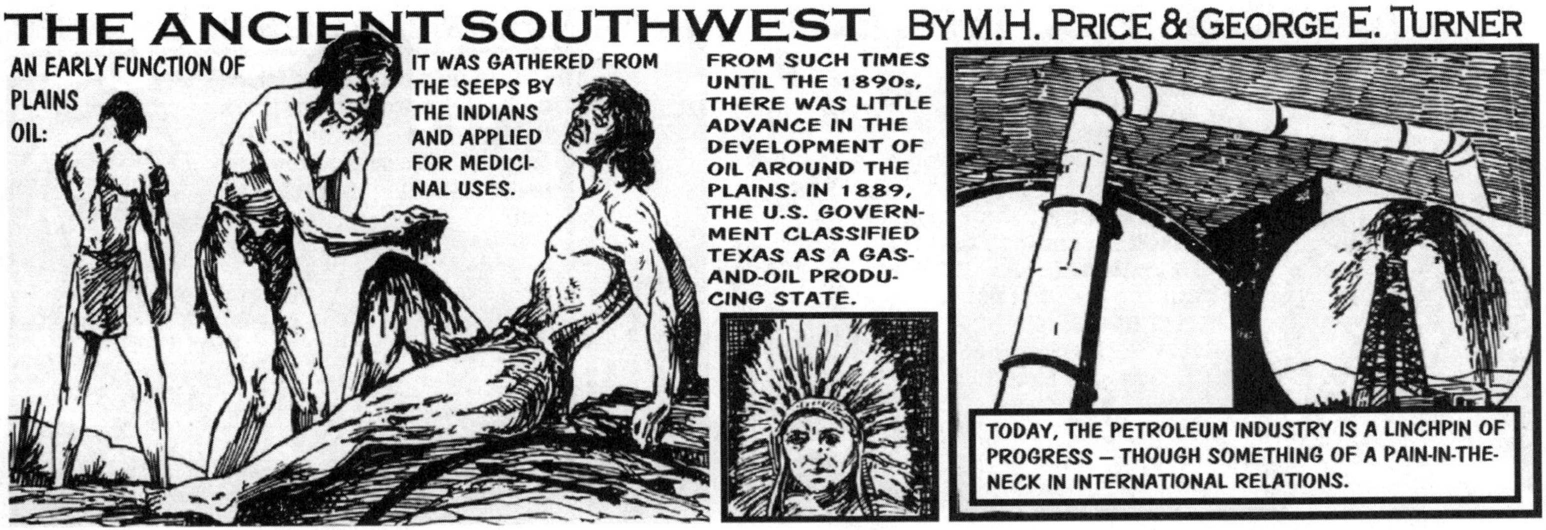
THE ANCIENT SOUTHWEST
BY M.H. PRICE & GEORGE E. TURNER
AN EARLY FUNCTION OF PLAINS OIL:
IT WAS GATHERED FROM THE SEEPS BY THE INDIANS AND APPLIED FOR MEDICINAL USES.
FROM SUCH TIMES UNTIL THE 1890s, THERE WAS LITTLE ADVANCE IN THE DEVELOPMENT OF OIL AROUND THE PLAINS. IN 1889, THE U.S. GOVERNMENT CLASSIFIED TEXAS AS A GAS-AND-OIL PRODUCING STATE.
TODAY, THE PETROLEUM INDUSTRY IS A LINCHPIN OF PROGRESS — THOUGH SOMETHING OF A PAIN-IN-THE-NECK IN INTERNATIONAL RELATIONS.

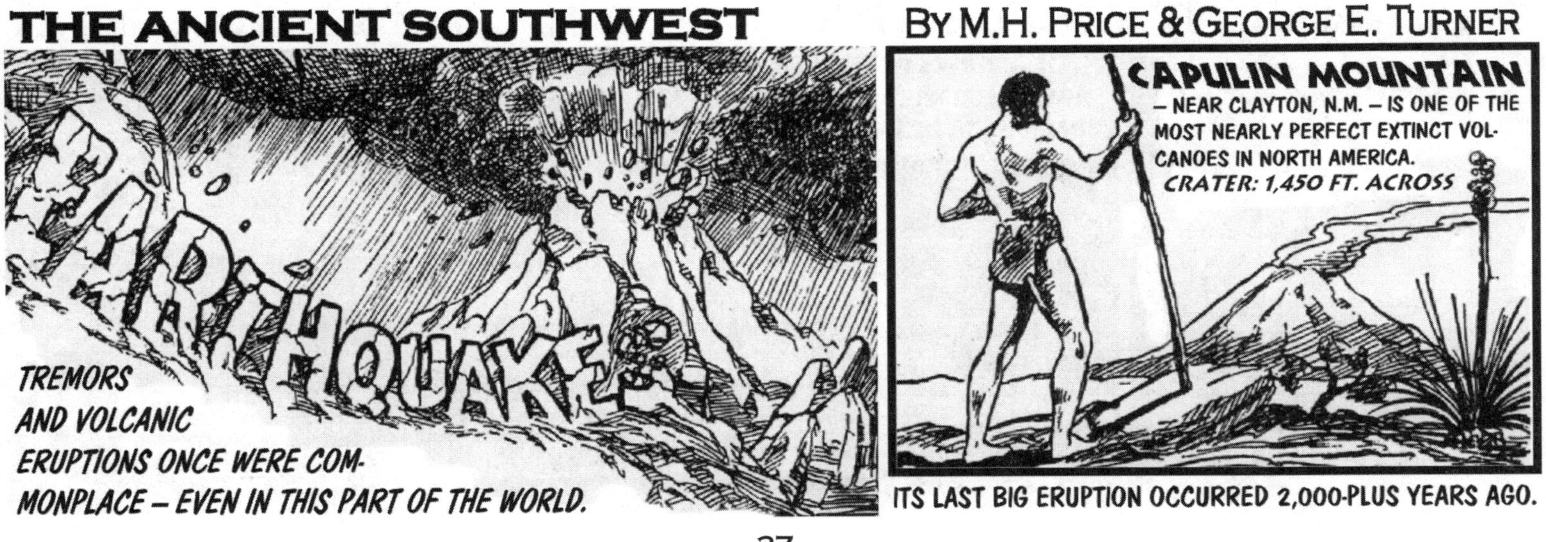
THE ANCIENT SOUTHWEST
BY M.H. PRICE & GEORGE E. TURNER
EARTHQUAKE
TREMORS AND VOLCANIC ERUPTIONS ONCE WERE COMMONPLACE — EVEN IN THIS PART OF THE WORLD.
CAPULIN MOUNTAIN
— NEAR CLAYTON, N.M. — IS ONE OF THE MOST NEARLY PERFECT EXTINCT VOLCANOES IN NORTH AMERICA.
CRATER: 1,450 FT. ACROSS
ITS LAST BIG ERUPTION OCCURRED 2,000-PLUS YEARS AGO.

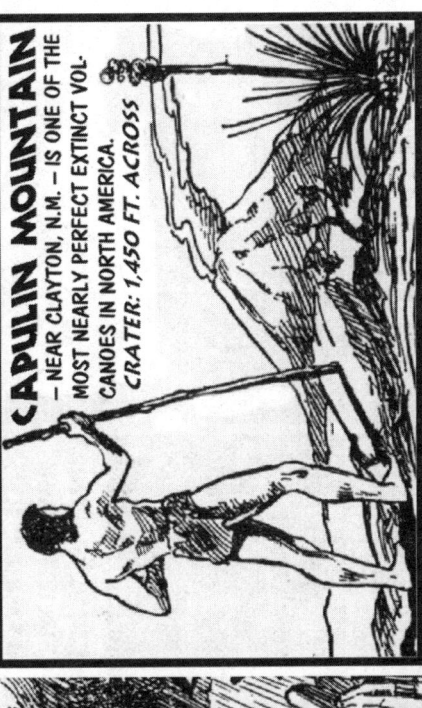

THE ANCIENT SOUTHWEST

By M.H. PRICE & GEORGE E. TURNER

Coronado

In his search for the Seven Cities of Gold, the explorer passed through Texas' Palo Duro region. Relics of his expedition — such as armor and pieces of livery — have been found.

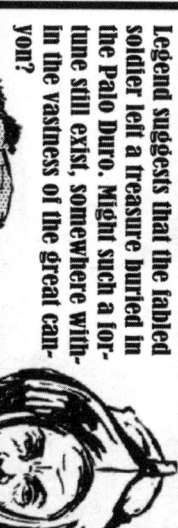

Legend suggests that the fabled soldier left a treasure buried in the Palo Duro. Might such a fortune still exist, somewhere within the vastness of the great canyon?

YEAH, RIGHT.

THE ANCIENT SOUTHWEST

By M.H. PRICE & GEORGE E. TURNER

All features of our present-day landscapes have been shaped during the past 60 million years — the last three per cent of geologic time.

During this time, the rivers found their courses; climatic regions were established; the mountains rose to their present levels; and the shorelines were fixed.

NEXT WEEK:
The Palo Duro Story

THE PALO DURO STORY

THE PALO DURO STORY

BY M.H. PRICE & GEORGE E. TURNER

It is unfortunate that the towering walls and eerie rock formations of "The Grand Canyon of Texas" cannot talk — to tell us of the many astonishing tales that have been enacted there. In this series — with the aid of some dramatic license — we will attempt a retelling.

A Weekly Vignette

GREED

BY M.H. PRICE & GEORGE E. TURNER

It was a lust for gold that brought the flag of Spain to the Americas. With it came the first white men ever to see the grassy region that they would call el Llano Estacado — the Staked Plains.

Coronado was a man half-crazed with the desire for riches. Such madness drove him and a gigantic expedition...

... into an unplumbed wilderness, with strange consequences. The story begins unfolding next week.

THE PALO DURO STORY

To the superstitious expeditioners from Spain, America loomed in the imagination as a land of unknown terrors.

The earliest explorers had brought back tales of gigantic warrior-women, two-headed cannibals and fearsome monsters — among other wonders.

The more fantastic the tales, the more readily the nobility believed them — and made haste to experience this strange new world.

Then there was the promise of some Fountain of Everlasting Youth.

THE PALO DURO STORY

BY M.H. PRICE & GEORGE E. TURNER

Adventure? It was there in abundance. So was a forced confrontation with mortality.

Next: A Doomed Voyage

THE PALO DURO STORY   BY M.H. PRICE & GEORGE E. TURNER

During 1527-28, Panphilo Narvaez and Cabeza de Vaca head up an ambitious expedition to the Florida Coast. Narvaez orders his ships to go on to the *West Indies* to replenish supplies — leaving 300 men aground.

WELL, CABEZA DE VACA — WHAT ARE YOU GRUMBLING ABOUT *THIS* TIME?

YOU SHOULD NOT HAVE SENT THE SHIPS AWAY, NARVAEZ.

DON'T BE A FOOL, DE VACA. THEY WILL RETURN TO THE HARBOR WITH SUPPLIES, AND WE'LL MEET THEM THERE. WHY SO WORRIED?

WELL, MAINLY BECAUSE WE DON'T KNOW THERE *IS* ANY HARBOR.

Next: From Bad to Worse

THE PALO DURO STORY   BY M.H. PRICE & GEORGE E. TURNER

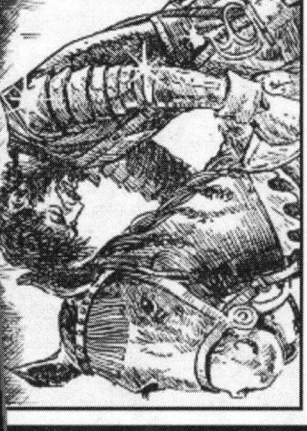

1528:

LET'S SEE, NOW — YOU SEND THE SHIPS AWAY FOR SUPPLIES, WITH ORDERS TO MEET US AT A HARBOR THAT NO ONE HAS ACTUALLY SEEN...

SO WHO APPOINTED YOU BOSS?

HIS MAJESTY, THAT'S WHO.

"AND I SAY WE GO MARCHING IN AS IF WE OWNED THE LAND."

Mere days later, the arrogant Cmdr. Narvaez comprehends his mistake: "We are being destroyed by the land we came to conquer! ...I cannot bear to think of dying in this unholy place!"

Next: Mutiny?

THE PALO DURO STORY

By M.H. Price & George E. Turner

1528: For days, Cmdr. Narvaez' embattled expedition slogs onward into Uncharted America, hoping to meet up with native residents — who have been stealthily following them all along.

The weary, starving refuse to give up.

I TELL YOU, DE VACA, OUR ONLY CHANCE IS TO GET RID OF NARVAEZ!

— ENOUGH OF YOUR MUTINOUS TALK, DORANTES!

Suddenly:

—VACA! WHAT'S THAT UP AHEAD? ANIMALS, OR —

— NO, BY HEAVEN! THEY'RE MEN!

NEXT: Welcome to the "New" World

THE PALO DURO STORY

By M.H. Price & George E. Turner

1528: At large in Uncharted America with a dwindling contingent of would-be conquerors from Spain:

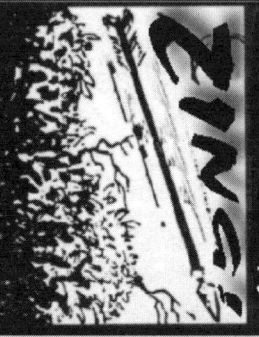

ZING!

Cabeza de Vaca calls out joyously to the silent figures in the shadows. The reply?

SEIZE THEM!

CLANK!

Their armor buys the intruders sufficient time to become fighting-mad.

"Alive!" shouts de Vaca. "Take them alive! They're of no use to us slain!"

NEXT: A Hostile Takeover

THE PALO DURO STORY

BY M.H. PRICE & GEORGE E. TURNER

1528:

QUICKLY! TO OUR BASE CAMP! TELL NARVAEZ WE HAVE CAPTURED SIX HOSTILE NATIVES!

An Indian siege upon Cmdr. Narvaez' expedition ends in victory for the well-armed invaders from Europe.

A forced march to the Indians' village, where the first order of business...

... is for the famished intruders to deplete the tribe's supply of grain.

NEXT: Madness Afoot

THE PALO DURO STORY

BY M.H. PRICE & GEORGE E. TURNER

1528: Expedition leader Narvaez becomes ever more of a liability to his conquering troops.

WE CANNOT GO ON LIKE THIS, DE VACA! NARVAEZ IS INSANE!

"HIS OBSESSION WITH FINDING SOME LOST TREASURE ALONG THE WAY — IT'S LEADING US TO DOOM!"

SHIPWRECKS — DROWNINGS — DISEASE — EVEN NOW, WE HAVEN'T ENOUGH HORSES TO HAUL THE DYING!

SILENCE! I WILL LISTEN NO FURTHER!

NEXT: Death Stalks the Explorers

-43-

THE PALO DURO STORY

By M.H. PRICE & GEORGE E. TURNER

1528: Cabeza de Vaca knows that his fellow explorer, Dorantes, is right about the madness of their commander and the dangers they all face.

And as the situation worsens, the only constant is...

DEATH... AGAIN AND AGAIN.

THE PALO DURO STORY

By M.H. PRICE & GEORGE E. TURNER

1528: Cmdr. Narvaez, now afflicted with the fever that has felled scores of his men...

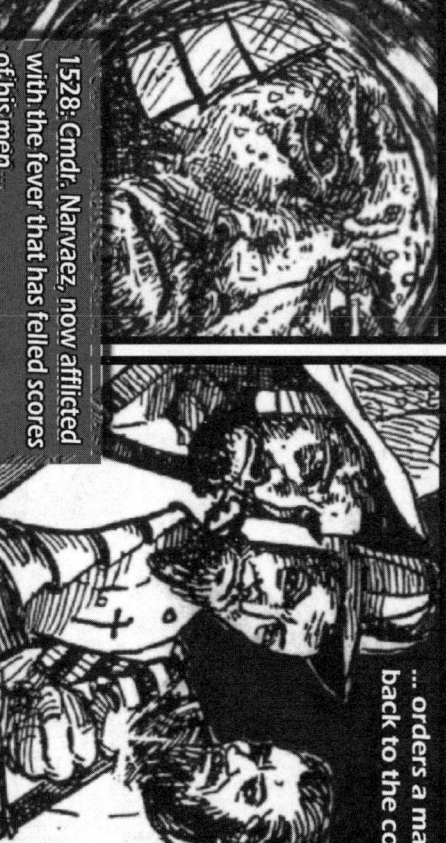

... orders a march back to the coast...

... in the hope of re-connecting with the ships he had sent away with the foolhardy assumption of an easy rendezvous.

There is no sign of ships, nor of harbor.

NEXT: A Crash Course in Shipbuilding

THE PALO DURO STORY

BY M.H. PRICE & GEORGE E. TURNER

1528:

And still mounts the toll of sickness-unto-death among the prospective conquerors.

An escape by sea seems the likeliest hope, and so it is decided to build boats enough to reach the Spanish settlements in Mexico. Their ignorance of shipbuilding is beside the point.

Next: Meltdown

THE PALO DURO STORY

BY M.H. PRICE & GEORGE E. TURNER

1528:

In a last-ditch bid to escape a hostile land, the explorers melt metal implements into nails and shipbuilding tools.

Sails are patched together from clothing.

Days pass — then weeks. Can they succeed?

NEXT: Well, Can They?

THE PALO DURO STORY

BY M.H. PRICE & GEORGE E. TURNER

The Spaniards struggle to build boats — their sole hope of leaving this accursèd Florida coast.

Every third day, a horse must be sacrificed as food for the sick and the workingmen.

IT IS NOT FAIR THAT WE SONS OF SPAIN SHOULD STARVE WHILE THE NATIVE HEATHENS FEAST!

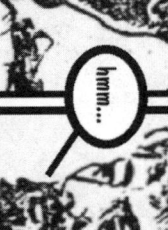

hmm....

NEXT: A Perilous Raid

THE PALO DURO STORY

By M.H. Price & George E. Turner

The interlopers raid the Indians' supply of maize.

A tribal council ponders the appropriate response.

Then, as a small group of explorers finds itself detached from the troops while gathering shellfish:

THE PALO DURO STORY

BY M.H. PRICE & GEORGE E. TURNER

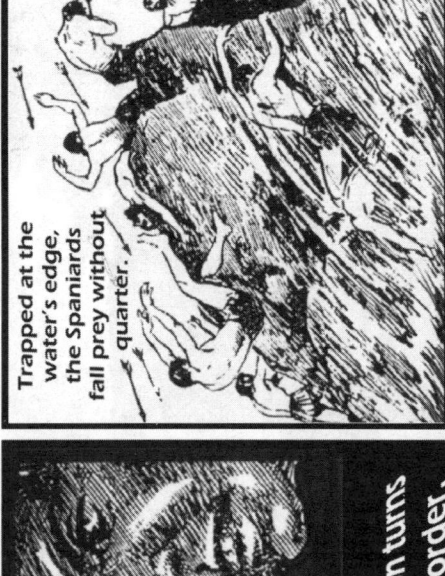

The Indians' indignation turns murderous in short order.

Trapped at the water's edge, the Spaniards fall prey without quarter.

NEXT: Seaworthy or Not...

THE PALO DURO STORY

BY M.H. PRICE & GEORGE E. TURNER

Some 50 men must be carried in each of the crude barges — which are only 30 ft. long. The sea is choppy, and the nearest Spanish settlement is 1,000 miles away.

Decimated by attacks and disease, the Spaniards prepare to set sail...

...only to realize that none of the survivors has any such experience.

NEXT: Taking the Plunge

THE PALO DURO STORY

BY PRICE & TURNER

Sept. 22, 1528: The remnants of Narvaez' expedition ship out in five hastily constructed boats, leaving the remains of 50 comrades and many horses.

Narvaez commands the first boat.

Cabeza de Vaca takes charge of another. All the boats are overloaded.

NEXT: All at Sea

THE PALO DURO STORY

BY M.H. PRICE & GEORGE E. TURNER

The sea grows rougher. Inasmuch as none of the men knows navigation, they stick to the coastline. Only a few inches of the sides remain above water.

NEXT: Not a Drop To Drink

THE PALO DURO STORY

BY M.H. PRICE & GEORGE E. TURNER

Cmdr. Narvaez' battered expedition follows the shoreline in search of a landing...

... which shows itself when least expected.

But on the horizon:

Next: The Storm Breaks

THE PALO DURO STORY

BY M.H. PRICE & GEORGE E. TURNER

HURRY, MEN! GET THOSE BOATS OUT OF REACH OF THE WAVES! NO WATER TO DRINK ON THIS ROCK, BUT AT LEAST WE WON'T **DROWN!**

The storm brings no fresh water — only wind-driven brine from the sea. Its fury mounts for almost a week as the explorers struggle to establish a temporary shelter.

Next: A Briny Draught for the Drinking

-49-

THE PALO DURO STORY

BY M.H. PRICE & GEORGE E. TURNER

To one maddened by thirst, sea water is irresistible...

... and several can only succumb.

Theirs is a ghastly end.

Next: Isle of Misfortune

THE PALO DURO STORY

BY M.H. PRICE & GEORGE E. TURNER

Some of the men go mad from thirst during their stay on *la Isla de Malhado* — the Island of Misfortune.

Despite the raging winds, the survivors decide to set sail again.

Once again, the clumsy barques meet a treacherous sea.

The five groups soon lose sight of one another.

NEXT: "Throw Us a Rope!"

BY M.H. PRICE & GEORGE E. TURNER

Narvaez proves his mettle as a leader of men:

KEEP GOING, MEN! WE'LL MAKE OUR WAY — SOMEHOW!

YOU'RE ON YOUR OWN!

NEXT:
An Unexpected Welcome

THE PALO DURO STORY

Vaca's party catches up with Narvaez' boat.

THROW US A ROPE! WE CAN KEEP UP — IF YOU'LL HELP US!

BY M.H. PRICE & GEORGE E. TURNER

Indians bring water and food. Narvaez presents the rescuers with gifts. There are fires, for warmth and cooking. Soon, the explorers have drifted off to sleep.

NEXT: Attack!

THE PALO DURO STORY

As evening falls, the storm-rocked boats safely reach the Bay of Pensacola.

-51-

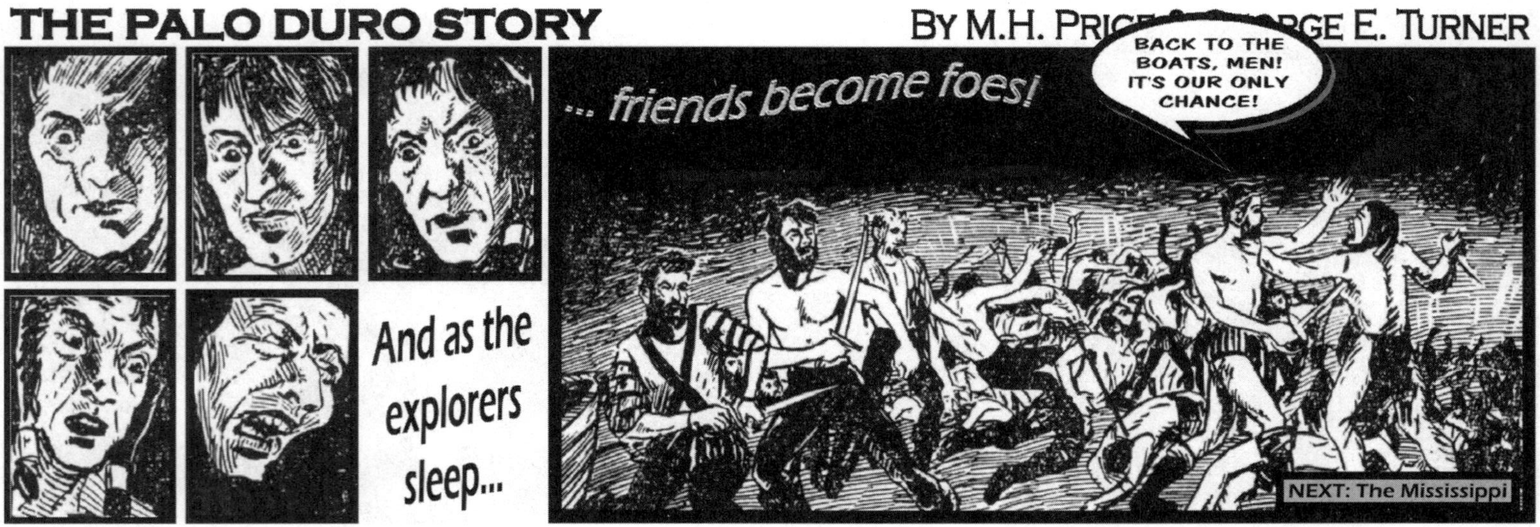
THE PALO DURO STORY
BY M.H. PRICE & GEORGE E. TURNER
And as the explorers sleep...
... friends become foes!
BACK TO THE BOATS, MEN! IT'S OUR ONLY CHANCE!
NEXT: The Mississippi

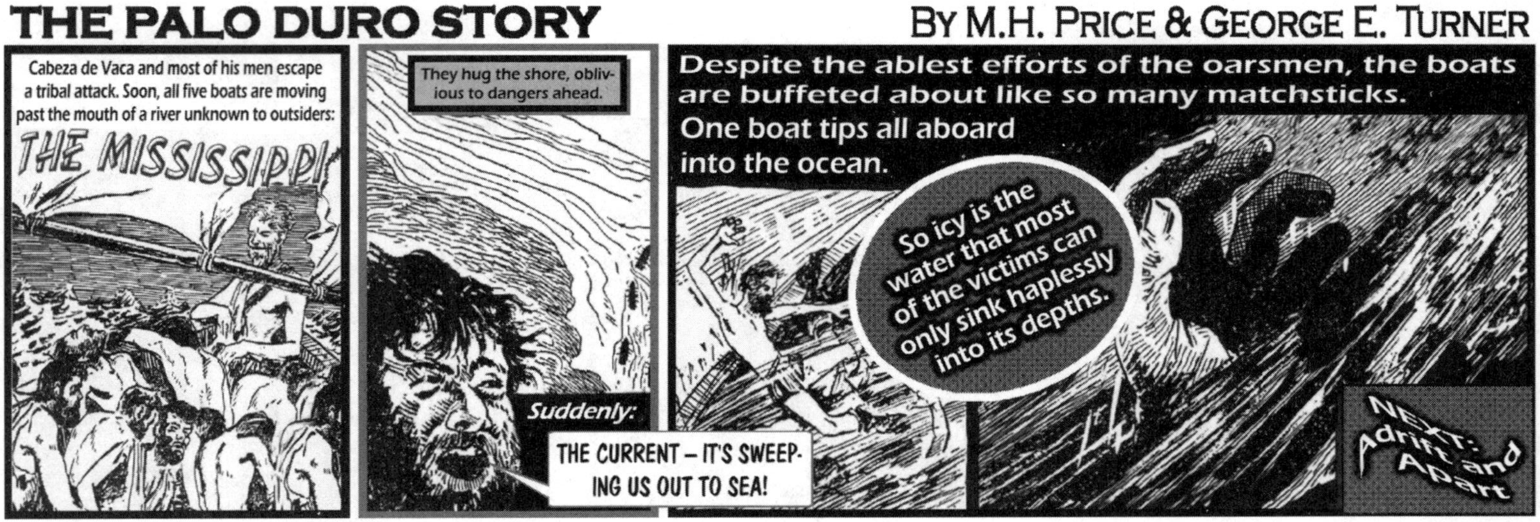
THE PALO DURO STORY
BY M.H. PRICE & GEORGE E. TURNER
Cabeza de Vaca and most of his men escape a tribal attack. Soon, all five boats are moving past the mouth of a river unknown to outsiders:
THE MISSISSIPPI
They hug the shore, oblivious to dangers ahead.
Suddenly:
THE CURRENT – IT'S SWEEPING US OUT TO SEA!
Despite the ablest efforts of the oarsmen, the boats are buffeted about like so many matchsticks.
One boat tips all aboard into the ocean.
So icy is the water that most of the victims can only sink haplessly into its depths.
NEXT: Adrift and Apart

THE PALO DURO STORY

BY M.H. PRICE & GEORGE E. TURNER

The currents of the mighty Mississippi allow few survivors from the wrecked boats of the Narvaez expedition.

Nightfall finds the boats becoming ever more scattered. The men on board feel horribly alone, wondering how such circumstances could have befallen the conquering sons of Spain.

NEXT: Crash Landing

THE PALO DURO STORY

BY M.H. PRICE & GEORGE E. TURNER

But as they approach, a mighty wave hurls the craft onto the beach.

CRASH!!

NEXT: Eyes in the Night

THE PALO DURO STORY

Cabeza de Vaca and his crew drift alone for a time, but eventually they find another of the boats. For four days, the two vessels stay together...

Rations run perilously low — mere handfuls of raw, sodden maize. As shore is again sighted, the few who are strong enough begin to row.

... but one night they drift apart again. Vaca's men fall unconscious, one-by-one, until only two are left to steer...

THE PALO DURO STORY

By M.H. PRICE & GEORGE E. TURNER

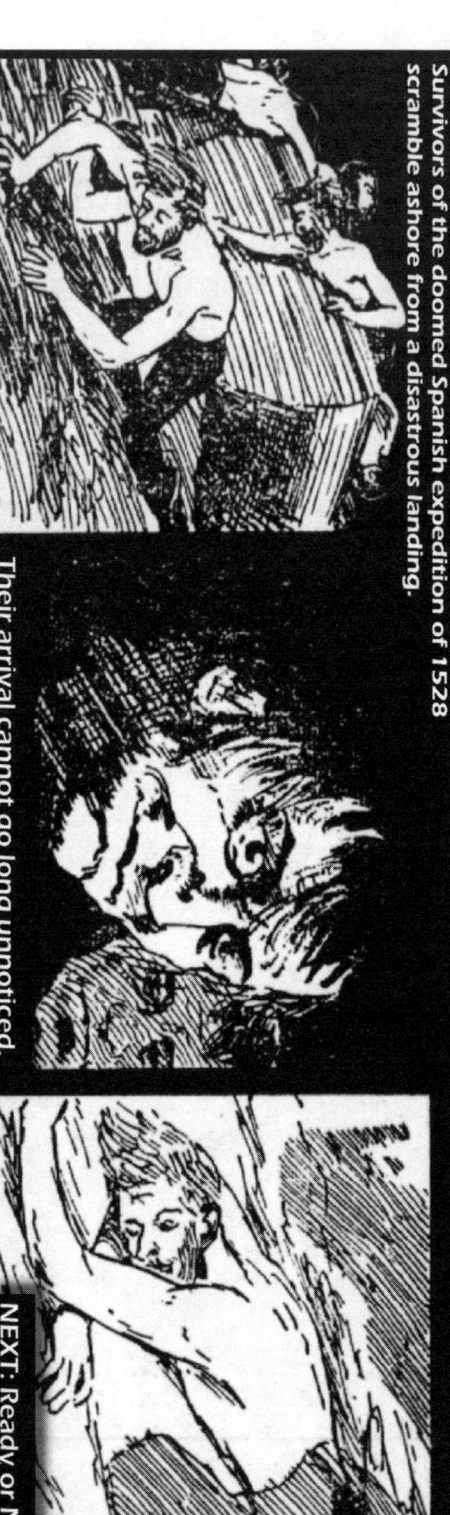

Survivors of the doomed Spanish expedition of 1528 scramble ashore from a disastrous landing.

Their arrival cannot go long unnoticed.

NEXT: Ready or Not...

THE PALO DURO STORY

After a harsh landing:

By M.H. PRICE & GEORGE E. TURNER

Such a display of hospitality catches the expeditioners off-guard, and susceptible to the Indians' helpful gestures. The crewmen, believing themselves doomed at any rate, prefer to stay on dry land. De Vaca, ever wary, presses for a hasty exit. Next: Out to Sea

THE PALO DURO STORY

By M.H. PRICE & GEORGE E. TURNER

De Vaca has no desire to win any popularity contests.

ENOUGH, ALREADY! PREPARE TO CAST OFF!

"Cabeza de Vaca," translated, means "Head of the Cow."

Seems de Vaca's leadership qualities may have been more of the bull-headed variety.

LOST IN AMERICA: 1528

Cabeza de Vaca's crewmen, relieved to be on dry land among apparently friendly Indians, balk at the idea of returning to a treacherous sea. De Vaca might have a mutiny on his hands if he neglects to assert his authority — here and now.

THE PALO DURO STORY

By M.H. PRICE & GEORGE E. TURNER

After first removing their clothing to avoid a soaking, Cabeza de Vaca and his crewmen launch their boat — only to capsize.

Food, clothing, provisions — all lost. The survivors can only struggle in the cold water, too numbed by the cold to swim.

Flung ashore, then, by another huge wave, they lie helpless as the Indians who had befriended them, now return. At the sight of such suffering, the Indians begin to weep and howl...

... and to build fires. Vaca fears that a cannibal feast may be imminent.

NEXT: Meanwhile...

-55-

THE PALO DURO STORY

By M.H. Price & George E. Turner

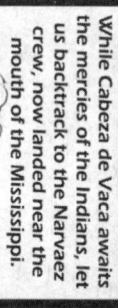

While Cabeza de Vaca awaits the mercies of the Indians, let us backtrack to the Narvaez crew, now landed near the mouth of the Mississippi.

All but Narvaez choose to bunk on shore. The commander remains aboard, with only a stone for an anchor.

A North wind carries the pitiful boat far out to sea.

Yes, and whatever his faults, Panphilo Narvaez, foolhardy leader of a doomed expedition, deserved a kinder fate.

NEXT: On the Coast of Texas

THE PALO DURO STORY

By M.H. Price & George E. Turner

#34

From last week: The disappearance of Cmdr. Narvaez. boat leaves this faction of the expedition with no means of escape from the wilderness they had sought to conquer.

While on an island off the coast of Texas...

Uncertain whether the Indians are their rescuers or their captors, the surviving crewmen have no choice but to wait.

A strange coincidence has found another boat of fellow expeditioners stranded on this same island. The reunited seafarers begin plotting a getaway.

By M.H. Price & George E. Turner

The boat captained by Dorantes and Castillo only looks seaworthy — it will not float.

NEXT: So Who's a Cannibal?

THE PALO DURO STORY

BY M.H. PRICE & GEORGE E. TURNER

Five survivors grow so fearful of starvation that they resort to a deed that can only appall the native tribesmen.

At the hands of the Indians, justice proves swift and final for those aristocratic sons of Spanish nobility who indulge in this cannibal feast.

NEXT: The Accursèd Settlement

Though kindly as a rule toward the captives, the Indians still harbor resentments that lead to the occasional killing.

Another plan is put into motion: Four swimmers will try for a Spanish settlement near Tampico. The bold effort fails as the couriers fall prey to the very wilderness they had sought to conquer.

THE PALO DURO STORY

BY M.H. PRICE & GEORGE E. TURNER

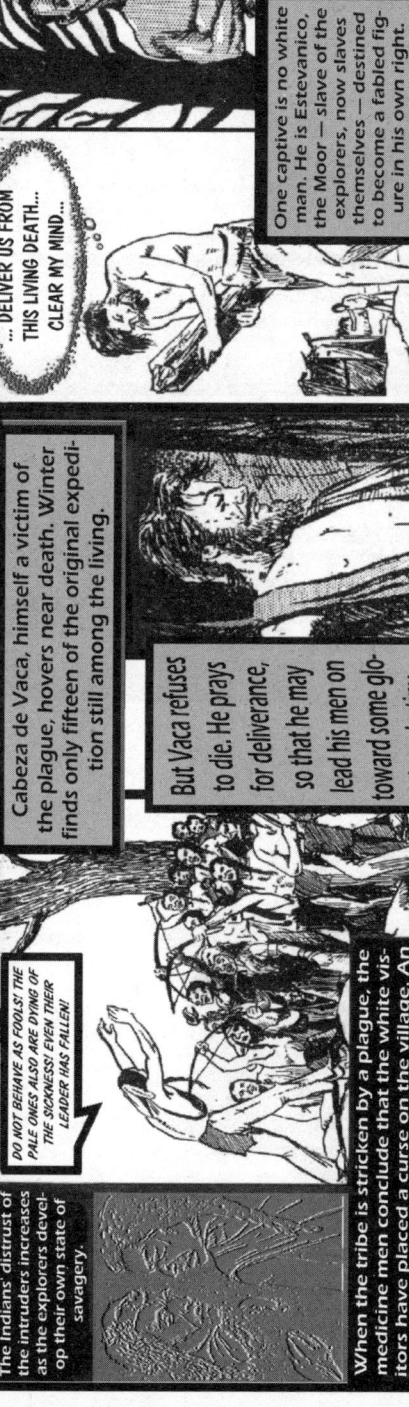

... DELIVER US FROM THIS LIVING DEATH... CLEAR MY MIND...

One captive is no white man. He is Estevanico, the Moor — slave of the explorers, now slaves themselves — destined to become a fabled figure in his own right.

NEXT: Enslaved!

Cabeza de Vaca, himself a victim of the plague, hovers near death. Winter finds only fifteen of the original expedition still among the living.

But Vaca refuses to die. He prays for deliverance, so that he may lead his men on toward some glorious destiny.

The Indians' distrust of the intruders increases as the explorers develop their own state of savagery.

DO NOT BEHAVE AS FOOLS! THE PALE ONES ALSO ARE DYING OF THE SICKNESS! EVEN THEIR LEADER HAS FALLEN!

When the tribe is stricken by a plague, the medicine men conclude that the white visitors have placed a curse on the village. An irate mob would do away with the Europeans, but one friendlier Indian intervenes.

THE PALO DURO STORY

BY M.H. PRICE & GEORGE E. TURNER

Each passing summer finds the captives from Spain settling into their enslaved condition.

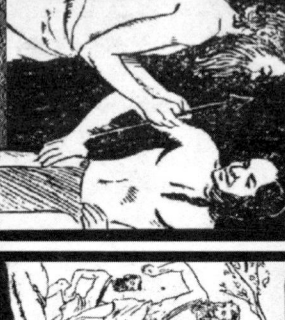

On the annual trips inland to feed on ripe prickly pear, the conquerors-turned-captives can see one another and compare notes. The year is now 1534.

They care little by now for de Vaca's insistence upon escape. Even de Vaca has gained a measure of freedom, as a craftsman and trader. But he persists...

... and so in the early autumn of 1534, the captives break free.

One crewman proves *lacking in courage.*

I CANNOT GO ON! I CAN FACE NO MORE OF THE UNKNOWN!

HE'S RIGHT! WHO KNOWS WHAT LIES AHEAD?

NO! OUR FAITH WILL LEAD US SAFELY ON!

Thus do America's first Christian doctors come into being — moving from place to place, healing the afflicted with simple prayer and common sense.

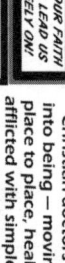

NEXT: Into Texas

THE PALO DURO STORY

The long and strange trek of Cabeza de Vaca winds inland, up Texas' Colorado River. The men pass the winter with a tribe of West Texas Indians.

Hardships — mostly from the Texas weather — remain, but these seem easy after the greater ordeals. And ever toward the sunset they move, finally in triumph.

BY M.H. PRICE & GEORGE E. TURNER

No longer slaves, but Children of the Sun. Worshipped by tribe after tribe, laden with food and gifts, they cross what are now known as the Sacramento and Diabolos Mountains.

NEXT: The Rio Grande

THE PALO DURO STORY

BY M.H. PRICE & GEORGE E. TURNER

Summer of 1535:

The four from Spain trek up the Rio Grande, welcomed now as kings and demigods. The gifts with which they are showered can only signify wealth ahead.

1536: They meet an Indian who wears a Spanish buckle upon his necklace. A frenzied search begins for fellow explorers.

Cabeza de Vaca finally locates a predatory company of Spanish slavers, to whom he appeals to leave his Indian friends in peace. The leader agrees — but then takes 500 Indians as slaves.

NEXT: De Vaca's Story

THE PALO DURO STORY

BY M.H. PRICE & GEORGE E. TURNER

"The story of Cabeza de Vaca is in-credible and would have to be con-sidered myth — except that it is true."

... so wrote Bernard de Voto in 1952's *The Course of Empire.*

Sure enough, Alvar Núñez Cabeza de Vaca was one of the most heroic adven-turers of all time. His exploits could fill a dozen movies and many more volumes of history.

In this series, we have shown highlights of his most famous travels, when he lived for eight years in the unplumbed vastness of Florida, Texas, New Mexico, Arizona and California.

After his rescue in 1536, Vaca went to Mexico and, at length, back to Spain. His chronicles convinced the Ruling Class of the potential for great wealth upon the North American con-tinent. In 1540, Vaca went to Brazil, for a new round of ad-ventures.

He was a man of kindness and charity — which made him a target of hatred dur-ing the cruel days of span-ism imperialism. Vaca was accused and convicted on a false charge in 1544 — imprisoned, then exiled to Africa.

His innocence was fin-ally established, and de Vaca returned with hon-ors to Spain, where he was appointed Judge of Seville. He lived to an advanced age.

SO THERE!

NEXT: A Strange Alliance

THE PALO DURO STORY

By M.H. Price & George E. Turner

Spain's bloody conquest of the Americas would continue under such butchers and thugs as De Soto, who killed Indians for the sheer sport of killing.

And meanwhile...

In Mexico, a strange alliance teams a priest, Fray Marcos, with deVaca's ally, the Moor Estevanico, on a search for wealth.

NEXT: Invasion

THE PALO DURO STORY

By M.H. Price & George E. Turner

The cruel sword of Spain has plunged deep into the heart of South America. The men from the Land of the Inquisition show a brutality beyond belief, committing atrocities to make the blood run cold.

NEXT: Marcos' Plot

THE PALO DURO STORY

BY M.H. PRICE & GEO. E. TURNER

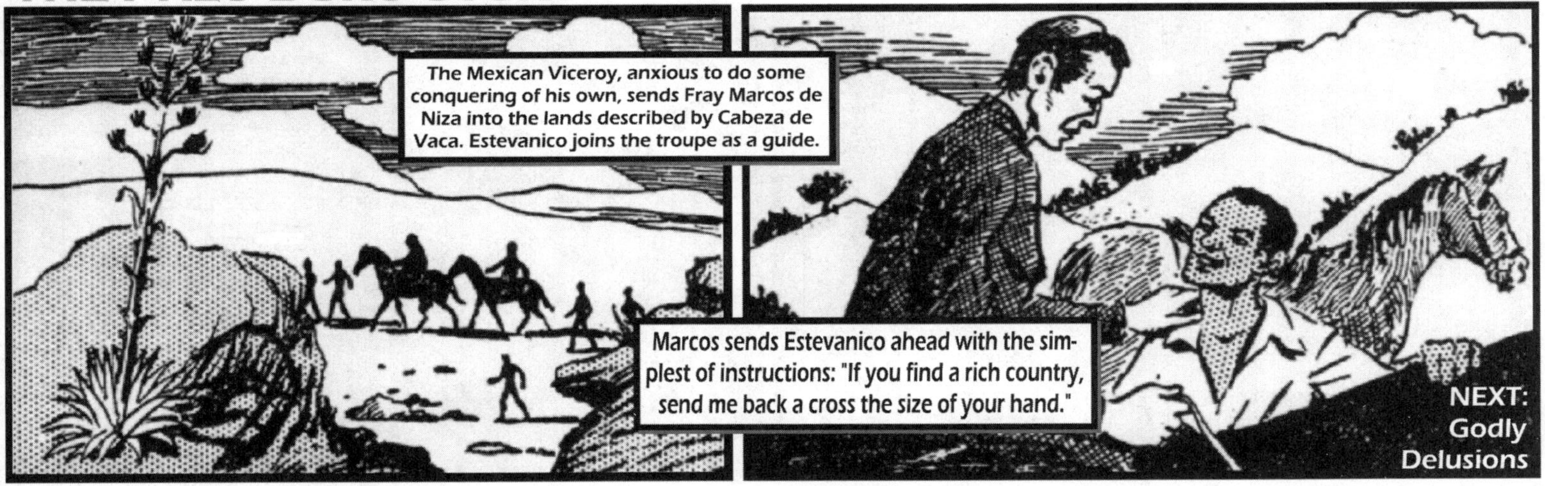
The Mexican Viceroy, anxious to do some conquering of his own, sends Fray Marcos de Niza into the lands described by Cabeza de Vaca. Estevanico joins the troupe as a guide.
Marcos sends Estevanico ahead with the simplest of instructions: "If you find a rich country, send me back a cross the size of your hand."
NEXT: Godly Delusions

THE PALO DURO STORY

BY M.H. PRICE & GEO. E. TURNER

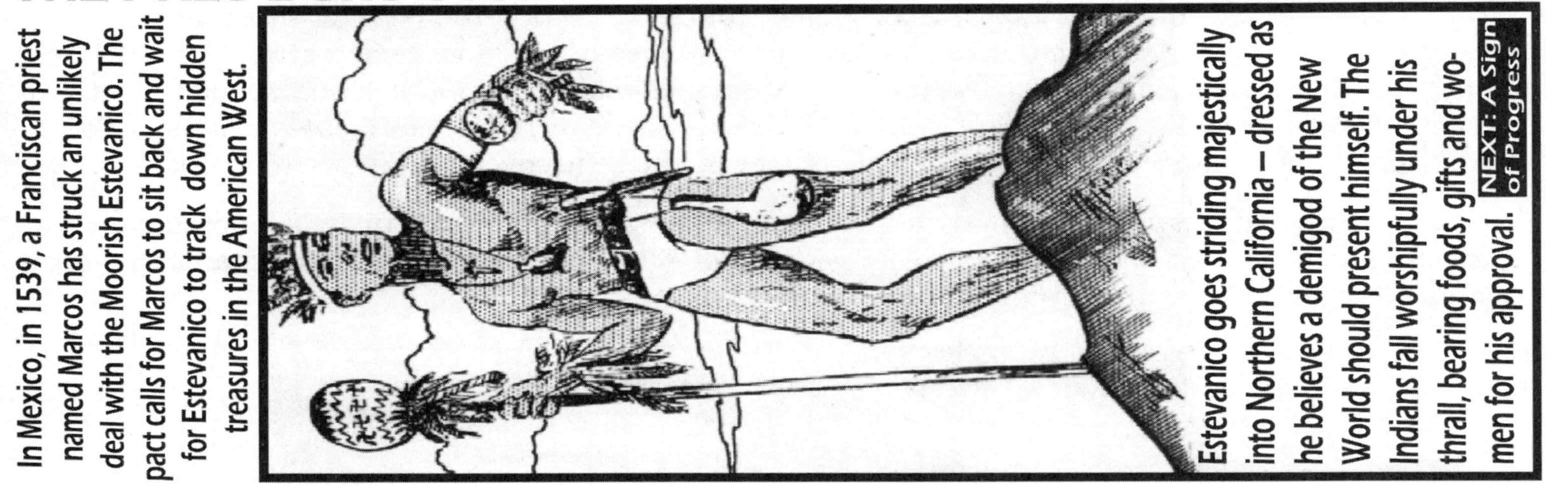
In Mexico, in 1539, a Franciscan priest named Marcos has struck an unlikely deal with the Moorish Estevanico. The pact calls for Marcos to sit back and wait for Estevanico to track down hidden treasures in the American West.
Estevanico goes striding majestically into Northern California – dressed as he believes a demigod of the New World should present himself. The Indians fall worshipfully under his thrall, bearing foods, gifts and women for his approval.
NEXT: A Sign of Progress

THE PALO DURO STORY

By M.H. Price & George E. Turner

Estevanico, the slave-turned demigod, thoroughly enjoys his job as Fr. Marcos' advance scout. The various tribes serve Estevanico's every whim.

If he finds evidence of treasure, Estevanico is to send back a seven-inch cross. He sends back a cross taller than a man! Marcos cannot wait.

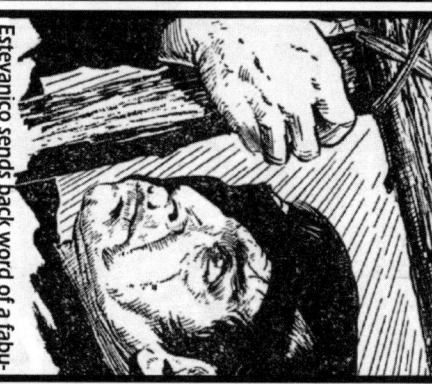

Estevanico sends back word of a fabulous city of gold — Cibola.

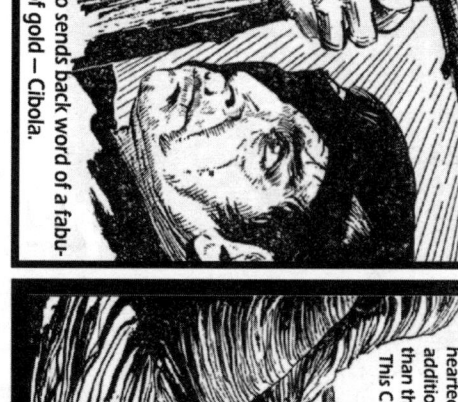
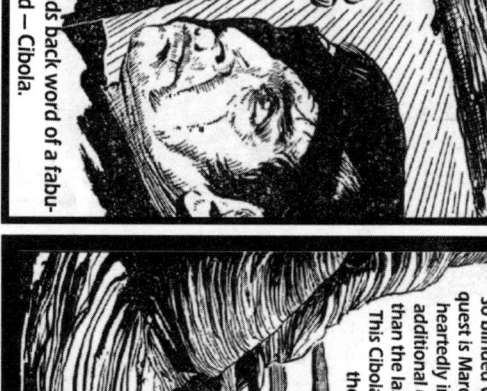

So blinded with the desire for conquest is Marcos that he buys wholeheartedly into the story. He finds additional crosses — each bigger than the last — all along the trail. This Cibola must be richer than the Aztec cities!

And here ends *The Palo Duro Story*, as originally conceived during the Pen-and-Ink Age and restored and reformatted during the Digital Age. Any promise of additional such strips can only be one of those Stories for Another Day—although I've seen considerable popular and scholarly acclaim for *The Ancient Southwest* in its recent revival as a recurring feature in *The Business Press of Fort Worth*. Sometimes, that Story for Another Day is merely the rediscovery of a story told long ago.

Meanwhile: Further such rediscoveries await, as gathered from George Turner's lengthy career as an aspiring schoolboy cartoonist, a collegiate gagman of gathering confidence, a commercial illustrator and overall a comics-struck storyteller.

—MICHAEL H. PRICE

JUVENILIA AND MARGINALIA

NOTES ON THE SELECTIONS

Old songs and older stories might not mean so much to some,

But those songs and older stories keep me close to those now gone...

—Texas balladeer GREG JACKSON

I had discovered the artistry of George E. Turner many years before I began working with him in the newspaper and cartooning trades. I was three years old when *The Ancient Southwest* surfaced in my hometown's Sunday newspaper, and the weekly feature promptly became my fourth- or fifth-favorite comic strip, alongside Vince Hamlin's *Alley Oop*, Chester Gould's *Dick Tracy*, Al Capp's *Li'l Abner* and Roy Crane's *Buz Sawyer*. My motivation to learn to read and to learn to relate what I might read to my surroundings was provoked largely by the funnypapers—particularly by those narrative serial comics that had more to do with adventurous struggles than with facile gag writing. *The Ancient Southwest* was a rare pleasure, inasmuch as it appeared only once a week. I sensed that this comic could not be taken for granted, and I used it as my introduction to a lifelong interest in natural history. The recognition that *Southwest* was of local origin, with its constant references to my native territory and its occasional nods to the wonderful Panhandle-Plains Historical Museum and its haunting relics of a gone world, only heightened the appreciation.

I soon learned that this Turner chap was pursuing a cartooning career vaster by far than just the newspaper strip. George is the first artist whose work I learned to recognize more by style than by signature: Various restaurants and tourist-trap curio shops around the Plains region carried a line of postal cards featuring unabashedly corny cartoons—often having to do with Texas-bred legends and stereotypes, such as the fabled Jackalope and horned lizards as big as elephants—and drawn in the style I had come to associate with *The Ancient Southwest*. These distinctive images were signed "Tex," or sometimes "Tex Lowell."

I filed that bit of trivia away for long-term reference, and when finally George and I crossed paths during the 1960s—he was chairing the Amarillo Film Society, whose programs I usually attended—I asked him, "So what do you hear from Tex Lowell these days?"

George seized the joke straightaway, muttered something about how that old coot Lowell hadn't been earning his keep lately, and then broke out laughing: "What makes you think I'm Tex Lowell?"

"Well, aren't you?" I replied, with all due schoolkid overconfidence.

"Well, I guess I am — but y'know, the reason us cartoonist guys give ourselves pseudonyms and secret identities, is to keep people guessing."

"No guesswork about it," I said. "Can't disguise the style."

I soon wound up working as a cub reporter in George's newsroom. He was just then beginning to compile a movie history book called *The Making of King Kong*, and that project became my apprenticeship apart from the city desk. By 1975, when the *Kong* book saw publication, George and I had launched into a fuller collaboration on a book known as *Forgotten Horrors*—a survey of low-budget movies from the Depression years.

George's background was a mixture of the rustic and the citified. Born in Burkburnett, Texas, to an oilpatch and ranching family, he had grown up in Amarillo (where his father, George A. Turner, had taken up a new career as a barber); then in Los Angeles; and then back in Amarillo. George found Amarillo provided a solid foundation of interests and operations, what with its extensive selection of first-run movie theatres—most of those managed by my maternal uncle, Grady L. Wilson—to say nothing of its central position in the heritage-rich Panhandle country, its receptive readership for George's words and pictures, and its proximity to some of the most striking geological formations this side of the Grand Canyon. From his base at the Globe-News Publishing Company, George helped to foster the preservation of the Alibates Flint Quarries, worked to protect the deeper reaches of the Palo Duro Canyon from overdevelopment and unrestricted tourism, and published an astonishing variety of stories and cartoons.

George had been delivering such a variety of work, for that matter, since childhood. The selections following come largely from George's younger days, beginning at the high-school level during the Depression-into-wartime years and continuing on through the first decade-and-change of his career in publishing.

—MICHAEL H. PRICE

From George Turner's high-school sketchbooks, a sequence of attempted storytelling. The long-unseen pages—affording a rare look at the creative process in embryo—surfaced during a largely futile search for original art from *The Ancient Southwest* and *The Palo Duro Story*.

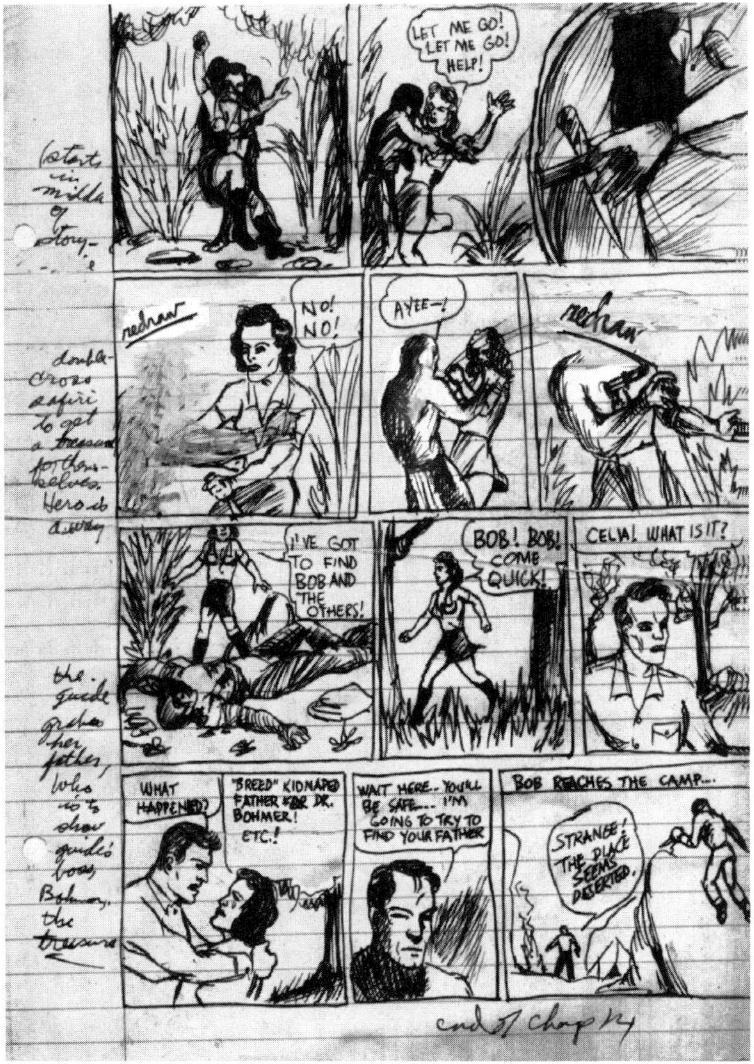
LET ME GO! LET ME GO! HELP!
redraw
NO! NO!
AYEE—!
redraw
I'VE GOT TO FIND BOB AND THE OTHERS!
BOB! BOB! COME QUICK!
CELIA! WHAT IS IT?
WHAT HAPPENED?
"BREED" KIDNAPED FATHER FOR DR. BOHMER! ETC.!
WAIT HERE... YOU'LL BE SAFE... I'M GOING TO TRY TO FIND YOUR FATHER
BOB REACHES THE CAMP...
STRANGE! THE PLACE SEEMS DESERTED.
end of chapter

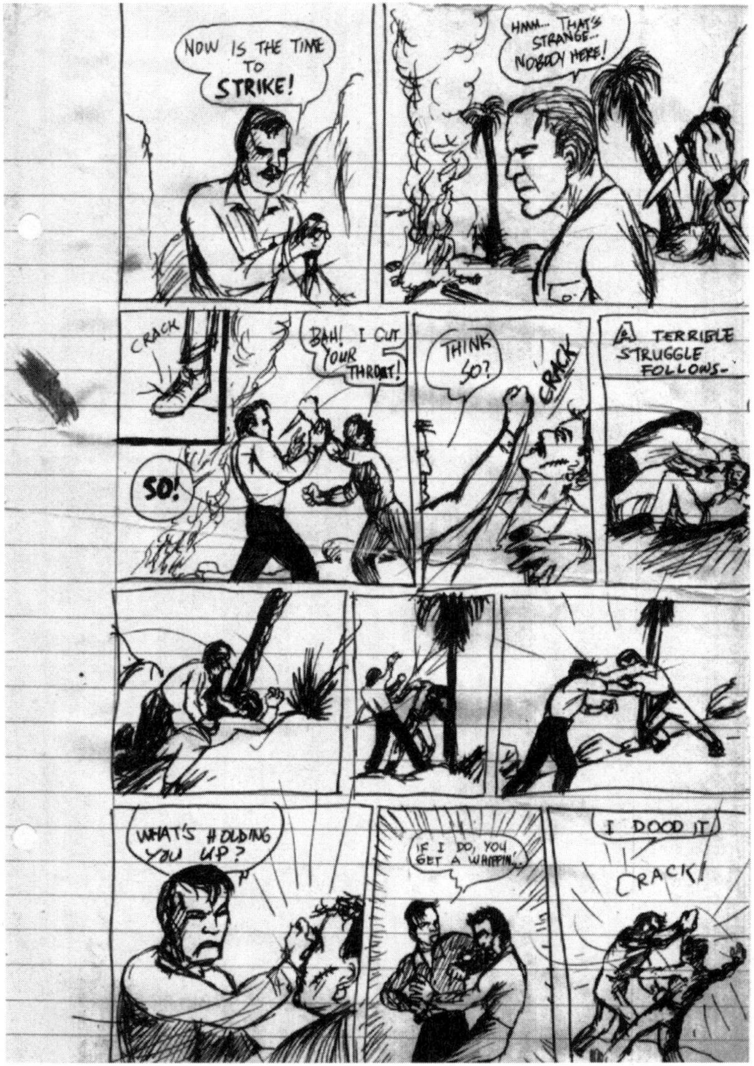
NOW IS THE TIME TO STRIKE!
HMM... THAT'S STRANGE... NOBODY HERE!
CRACK
SO!
BAH! I CUT YOUR THROAT!
THINK SO?
CRACK
A TERRIBLE STRUGGLE FOLLOWS—
WHAT'S HOLDING YOU UP?
IF I DO, YOU GET A WHIPPIN'.
I DOOD IT
CRACK!

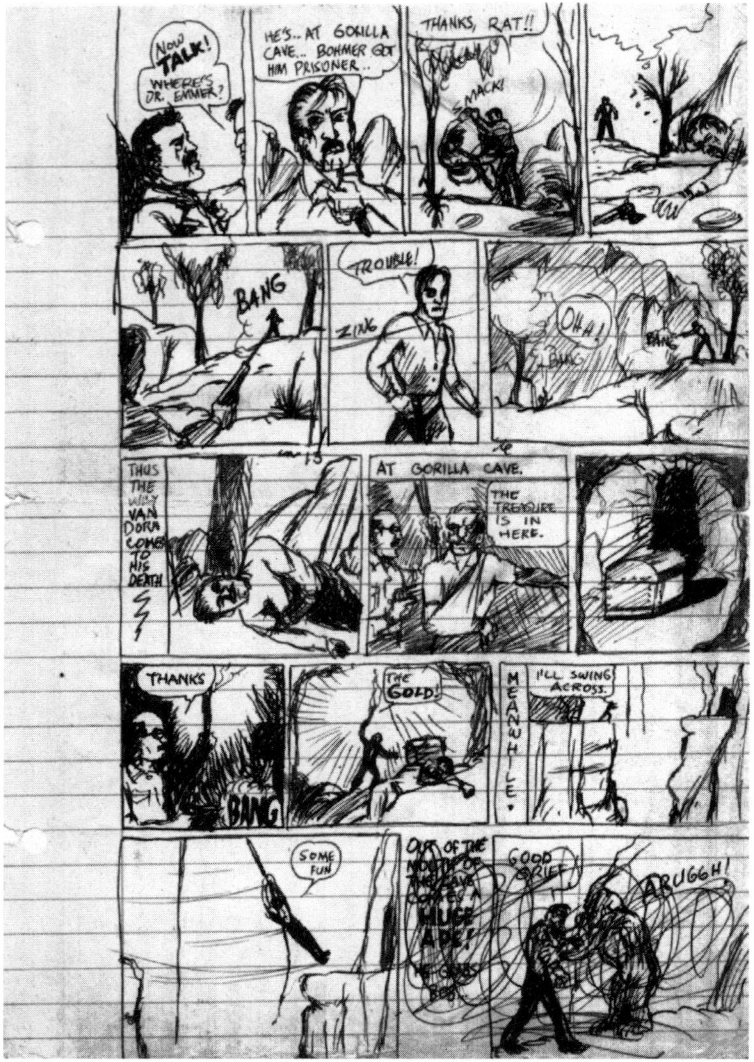
NOW TALK! WHERE'S DR. EMMER?
HE'S.. AT GORILLA CAVE... BOHMER GOT HIM PRISONER..
THANKS, RAT!!
SMACK!
BANG
TROUBLE!
ZING
OH!
BANG
THUS THE WAY VAN DORA COMES TO HIS DEATH
AT GORILLA CAVE.
THE TREASURE IS IN HERE.
THANKS
BANG
THE GOLD!
MEANWHILE.
I'LL SWING ACROSS.
SOME FUN
OUT OF THE MOUTH OF THE CAVE COMES A HUGE APE! HE GRABS BOB...
GOOD GRIEF
ARUGGH!

LIKE A SPIDER WATCHING A FLY, A HUGE APE FOLLOWS BOB...
BOB GOES IN, UNAWARE OF A HEAVY FIGURE FOLLOWING...
BOHMER COMING OUT...
TRENT!
BOHMER DUCKS INTO THE SHADOW IN TIME TO SEE THE GORILLA POUNCE ON BOB...
BOB THRUSTS THE FLAMING TORCH INTO THE GORILLA'S FACE.
THE GORILLA HITS BOB...
THE APE DRAGS BOB TOWARD THE ENTRANCE OF THE CAVE.....
OHH... MY HEAD..!! THE GORILLA! WHAT CAN I DO?!
ARRUGH!! ARUGH!
GOOD GOSH!
.. GOTTA HANG ON.. UGH—

THE PRAIRIE

VOICE OF STUDENT OPINION

West Texas State College

Canyon, Texas

REPRESENTED FOR NATIONAL ADVERTISING BY

National Advertising Service, Inc.

College Publishers Representative

420 MADISON AVE.   NEW YORK, N. Y.

CHICAGO · BOSTON · LOS ANGELES · SAN FRANCISCO

SUBSCRIPTION RATES	
Regular Session	$1.00
Semester	.50
Summer	.50

Published each Tuesday of the regular college year except during holidays or examination periods by the Student Association; entered as second-class matter at the post office in Canyon, Texas, under the Act of March 8, 1879.

MEMBER OF THE TEXAS INTERCOLLEGIATE PRESS ASSOCIATION

STAFF

Editor	Johnnie Fay Creens
Business Manager	Jess Herbert Pipkin
Photographer	Tom Knighton
Society Editor	Mary Jim Vincent
Music Editor	Bill Latson
Book Editor	T. C. Brown
Cartoonist	George Turner

Editorial Assistants—Margaret Lair, Beverly Sue Baker, Bill Davis, Ikey Gillespie, Norman Ely, Frank Stallings, James Harder, Betty Milton, Joyce Kessinger, Bascom Nelson, Don Turner, Magye Culwell, Gertrude Noe, Joe Page, Robert Sweny, Anne Beth Grigsby, Marvin Merrill.

Movie Memoir
("SON of KONG"
RKO—1933)

"JUNIOR! STOP PLAYING WITH YOUR FOOD!"

(PARAPHRASE an an oldie by R. TAYLOR) This Month: LINCOLN'S BIRTHDAY

LINCOLN STUDYING

LISTEN, POP—
ART IS ONE THING
—LIFE ANOTHER

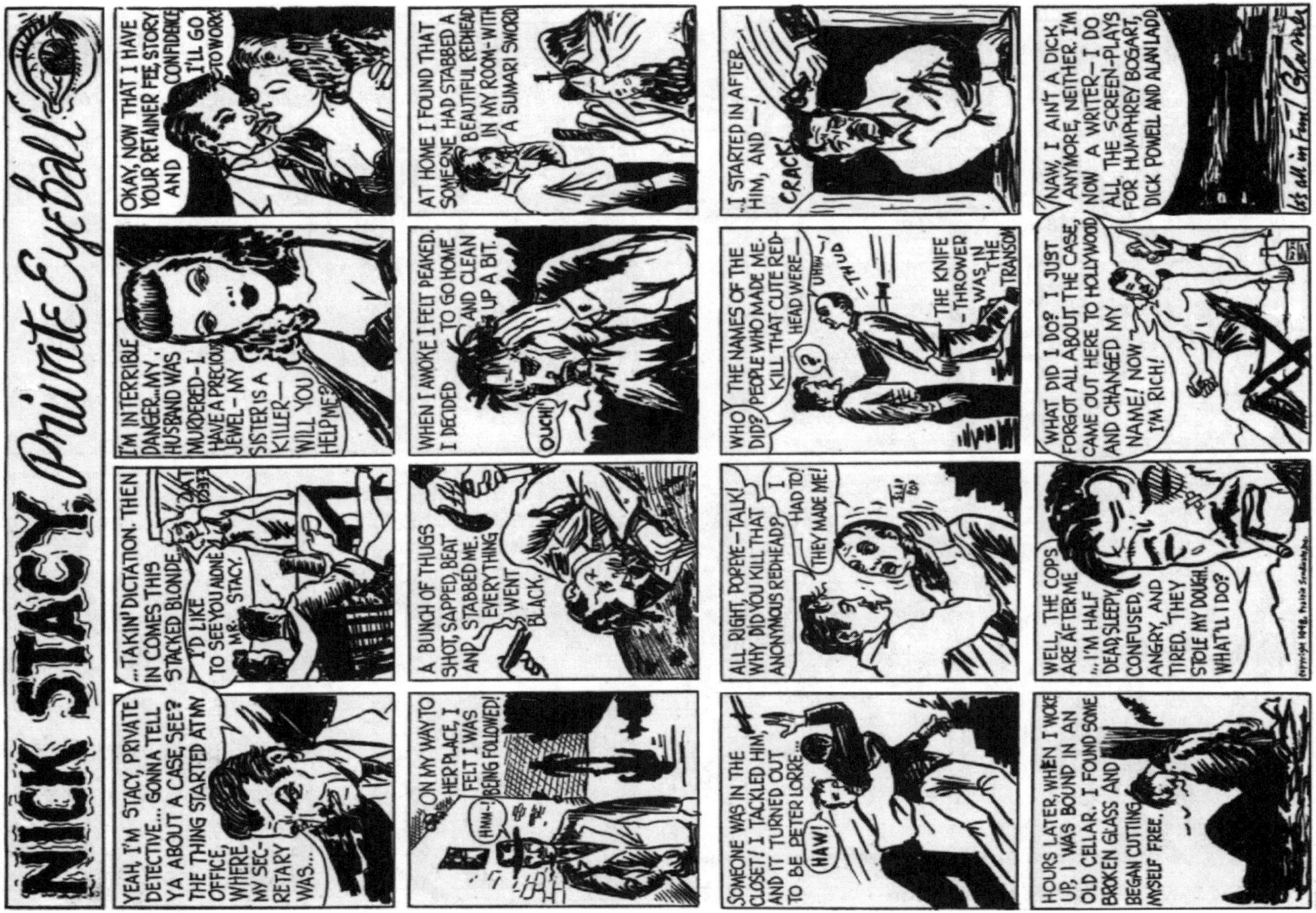
NICK STACY, Private Eyeball
YEAH, I'M STACY, PRIVATE DETECTIVE... GONNA TELL YA ABOUT A CASE, SEE? THE THING STARTED AT MY OFFICE, WHERE MY SEC-RETARY WAS...
...TAKIN' DICTATION. THEN IN COMES THIS STACKED BLONDE.
I'D LIKE TO SEE YOU ALONE MR. STACY.
I'M IN TERRIBLE DANGER...MY HUSBAND WAS MURDERED–I HAVE A PRECIOUS JEWEL–MY SISTER IS A KILLER–WILL YOU HELP ME?
OKAY, NOW THAT I HAVE YOUR RETAINER FEE, STORY AND CONFIDENCE I'LL GO TO WORK!
ON MY WAY TO HER PLACE, I FELT I WAS BEING FOLLOWED!
HMM–!
A BUNCH OF THUGS SHOT, SAPPED, BEAT AND STABBED ME. EVERYTHING WENT BLACK.
WHEN I AWOKE I FELT PEAKED. I DECIDED TO GO HOME AND CLEAN UP A BIT.
OUCH!
AT HOME I FOUND THAT SOMEONE HAD STABBED A BEAUTIFUL REDHEAD IN MY ROOM–WITH A SUMARI SWORD
SOMEONE WAS IN THE CLOSET! I TACKLED HIM, AND IT TURNED OUT TO BE PETER LORRE...
HAW!
ALL RIGHT, POPEYE–TALK! WHY DID YOU KILL THAT ANONYMOUS REDHEAD?
I HAD TO! THEY MADE ME!
WHO DID?
THE NAMES OF THE PEOPLE WHO MADE ME KILL THAT CUTE RED-HEAD WERE–
?
UHH–!
THUD
THE KNIFE-THROWER WAS IN THE TRANSOM
...I STARTED IN AFTER HIM, AND –!
CRACK!
HOURS LATER, WHEN I WOKE UP, I WAS BOUND IN AN OLD CELLAR. I FOUND SOME BROKEN GLASS AND BEGAN CUTTING MYSELF FREE.
WELL, THE COPS ARE AFTER ME ...I'M HALF DEAD, SLEEPY, CONFUSED, ANGRY, AND TIRED. THEY STOLE MY DOUGH. WHAT'LL I DO?
WHAT DID I DO? I JUST FORGOT ALL ABOUT THE CASE, CAME OUT HERE TO HOLLYWOOD AND CHANGED MY NAME! NOW–I'M RICH!
NAW, I AIN'T A DICK ANYMORE, NEITHER. I'M NOW A WRITER–I DO ALL THE SCREEN-PLAYS FOR HUMPHREY BOGART, DICK POWELL AND ALAN LADD

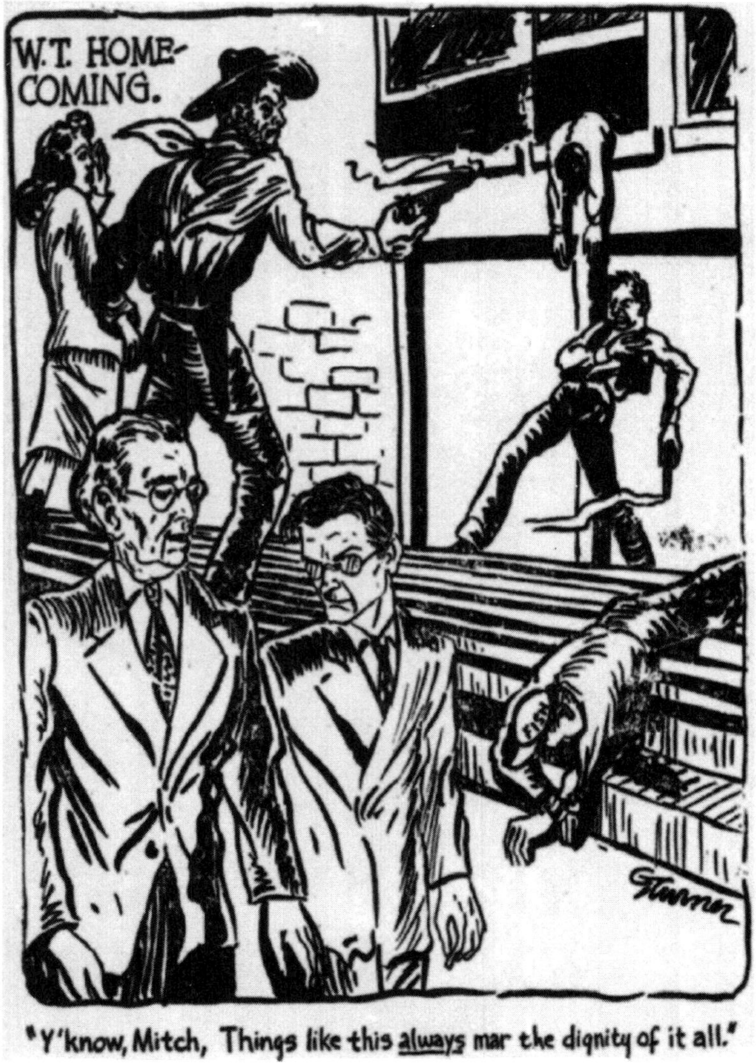
W.T. HOME-COMING.
Stanner
"Y'know, Mitch, Things like this always mar the dignity of it all."

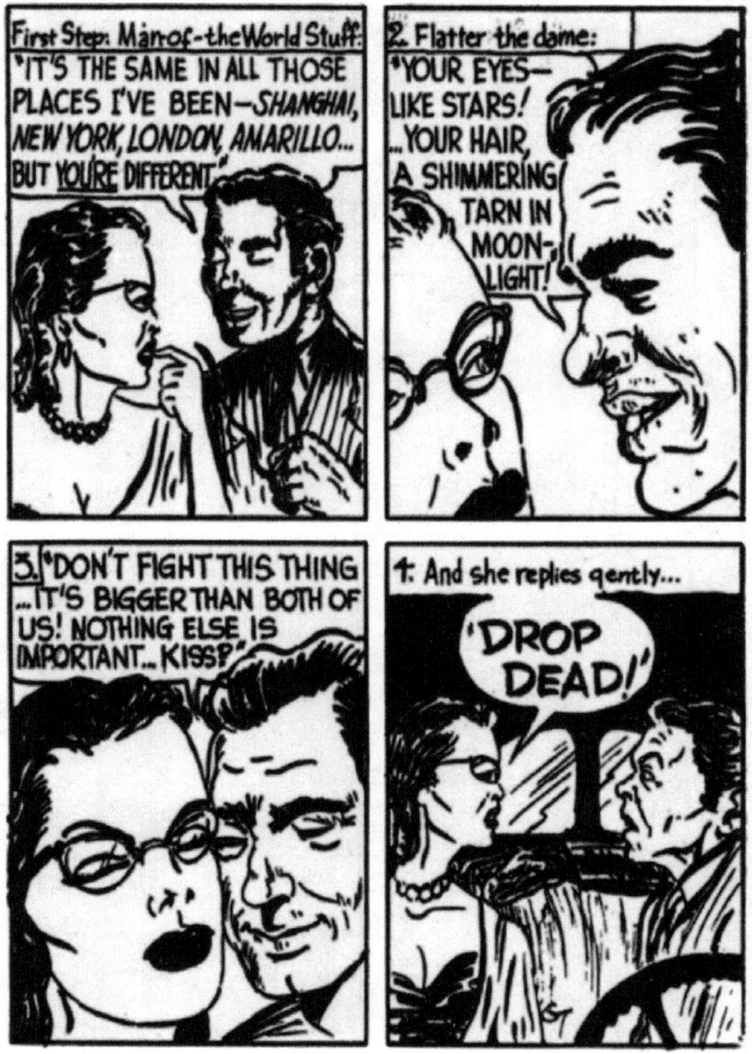
First Step: Man-of-the World Stuff:
"IT'S THE SAME IN ALL THOSE PLACES I'VE BEEN—SHANGHAI, NEW YORK, LONDON, AMARILLO... BUT YOU'RE DIFFERENT."
2. Flatter the dame:
"YOUR EYES—LIKE STARS! ...YOUR HAIR, A SHIMMERING TARN IN MOON-LIGHT!"
3. "DON'T FIGHT THIS THING ...IT'S BIGGER THAN BOTH OF US! NOTHING ELSE IS IMPORTANT... KISS?"
4. And she replies gently...
'DROP DEAD!'

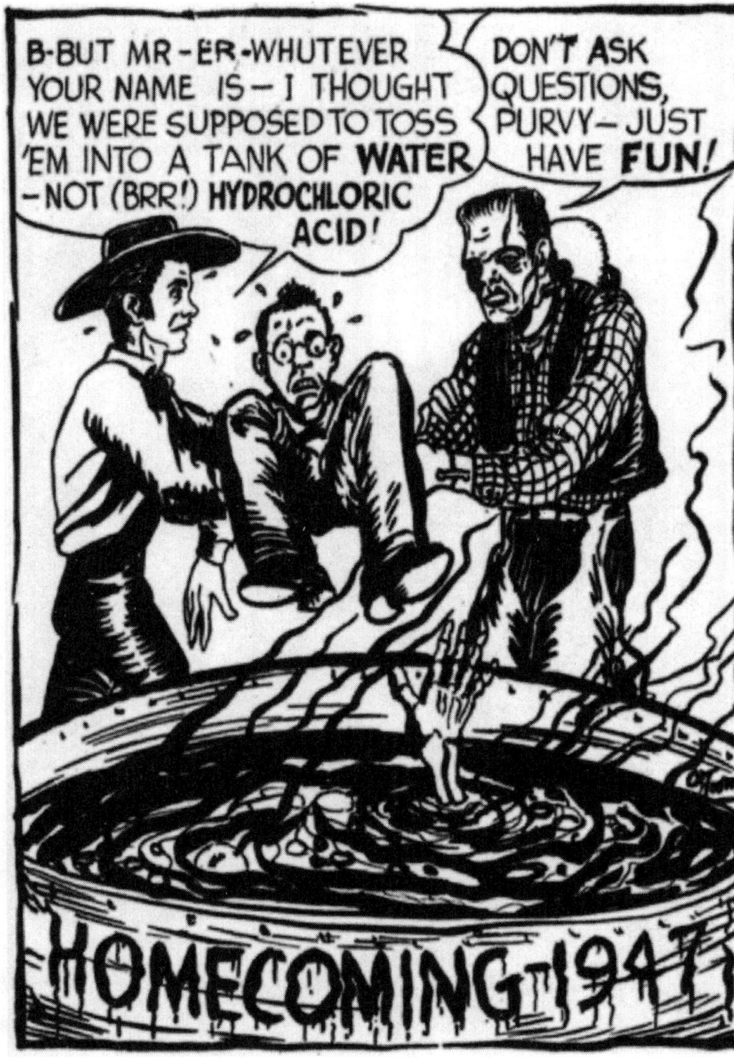

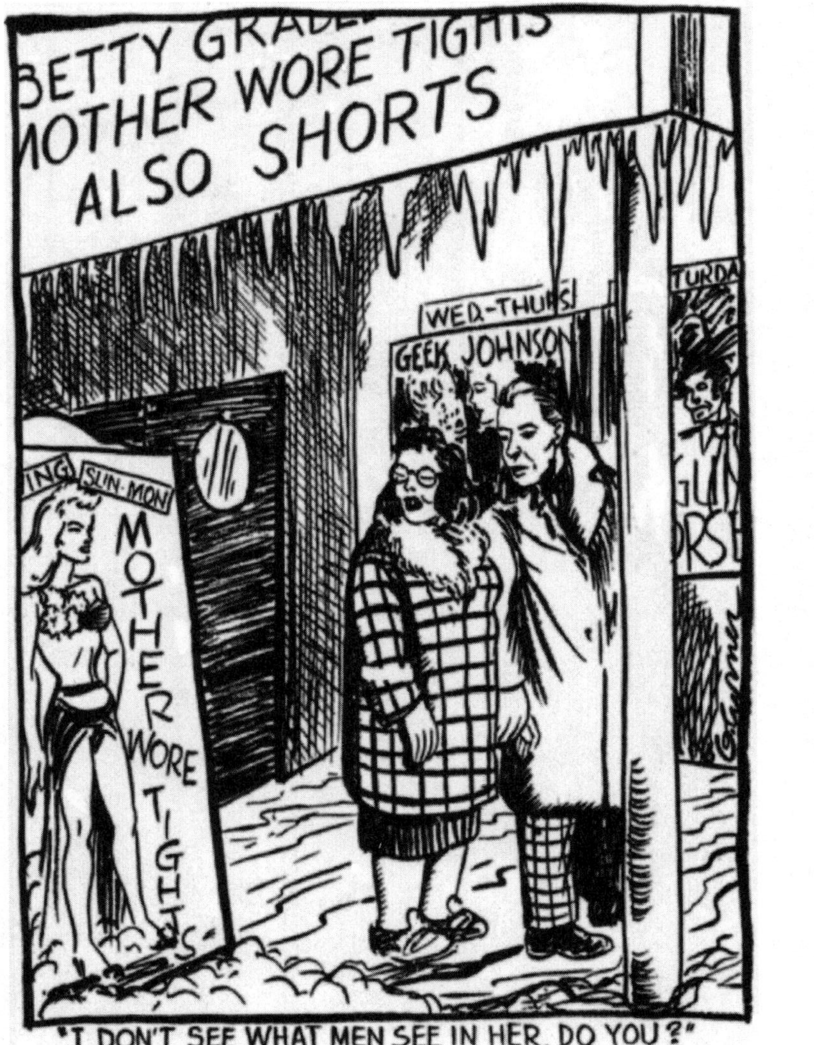

"I DON'T SEE WHAT MEN SEE IN HER, DO YOU?"

With apologies to Omar & Fitzgerald—

A book of Verse underneath the bough,
A loaf of bread, a jug of wine
and ... ah, wine ... we cannot
attain everything!

I DUNNO -- I THINK THEY'RE TECH STUDENTS WHO CAME DOWN FOR THE PIRATES' DANCE LAST WEEK

YOUR REFLEXES ARE NORMAL, MISS FLUBB.
MEDICAL DE
Dr. Ignatz Urp
copyright 1802 Joe Miller Syndicate Inc.

WELL, WELL! IF IT ISN'T MY OLD BUDDY TODDY GRUNCH!
ALL BEDDED DOWN WITH STREP THROAT, EH TODDY?
I MUST SAY YOUR THROAT DON'T LOOK AT ALL NECKED—HA HA,
GET IT?—STRIP, THROAT, NECK, NAKED-YAK, YAK, KUK, HAW!
BOY, ARE YOU LUCKY TO BE IN THIS NICE, WARM HOSPITAL! OUT
OF THIS WINDY WEATHER! MAN, IT'S ROUGH OUT THERE! YA
THINK I COULD GET A ROOM IN HERE FOR AWHILE, TODDY? YAK!
NO DULL TIMES FOR OLD TODDY WHEN HIS OLD BUDDY BOB IS
AROUND, EH, TODDY? YAK YAK! SAY, DID I TELL YOU ABOUT THE
GAL I WAS WITH
LAST NIGHT?
BOY, WHAT A
ETC. ETC.
BLAH—
Dedicated to everyone who has ever been in bed!

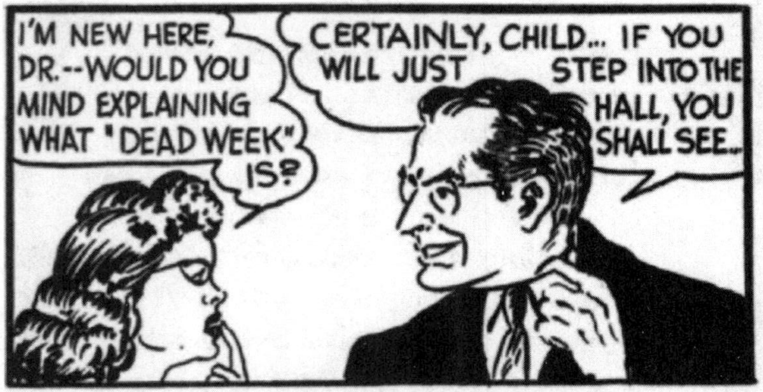
I'M NEW HERE, DR.--WOULD YOU MIND EXPLAINING WHAT "DEAD WEEK" IS?
CERTAINLY, CHILD... IF YOU WILL JUST STEP INTO THE HALL, YOU SHALL SEE...

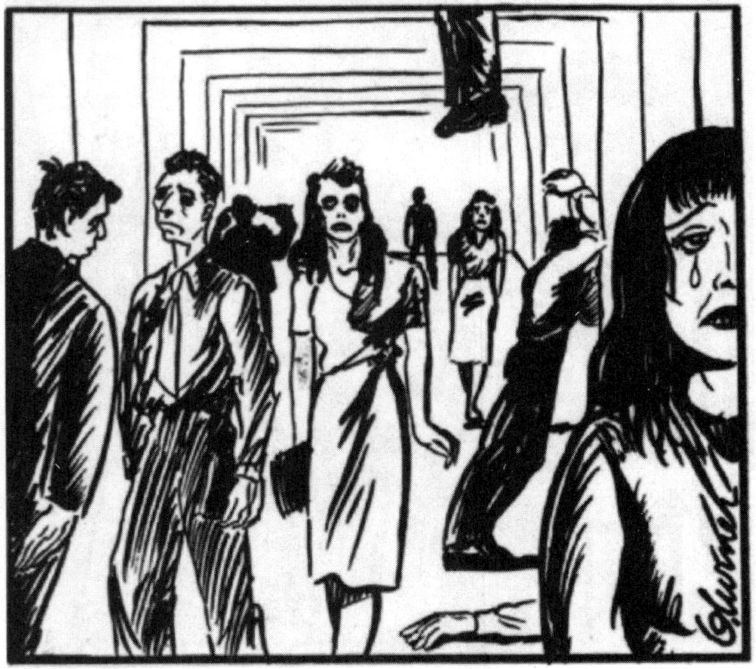

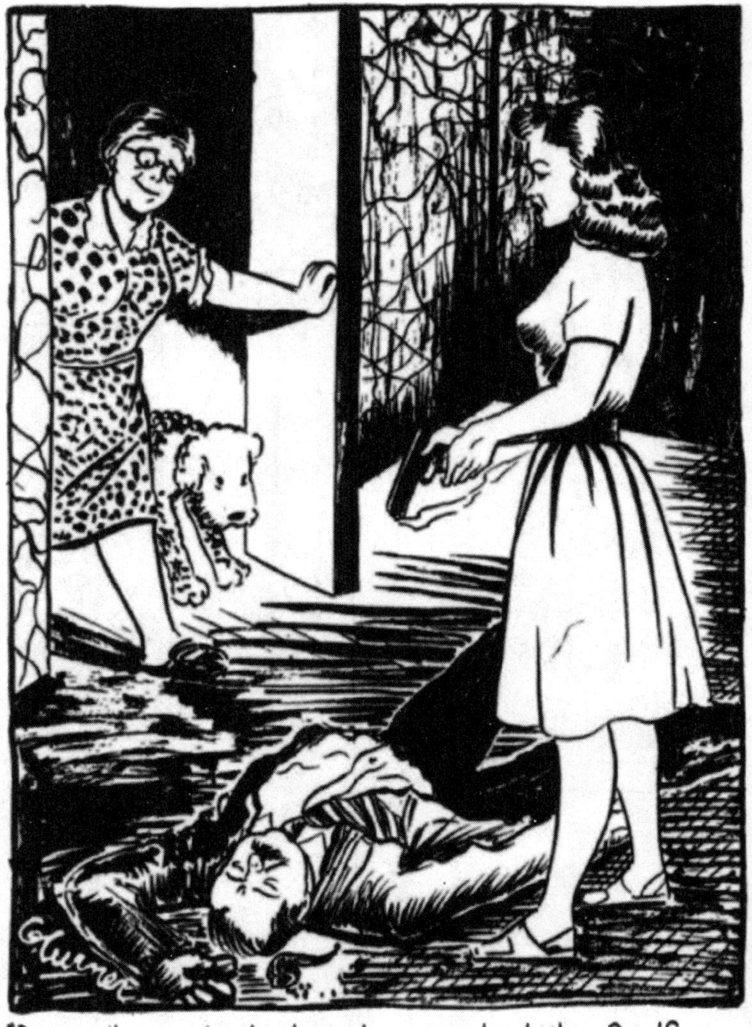

"Don't tell me you lovebirds are having another little — Oops! Sorry...

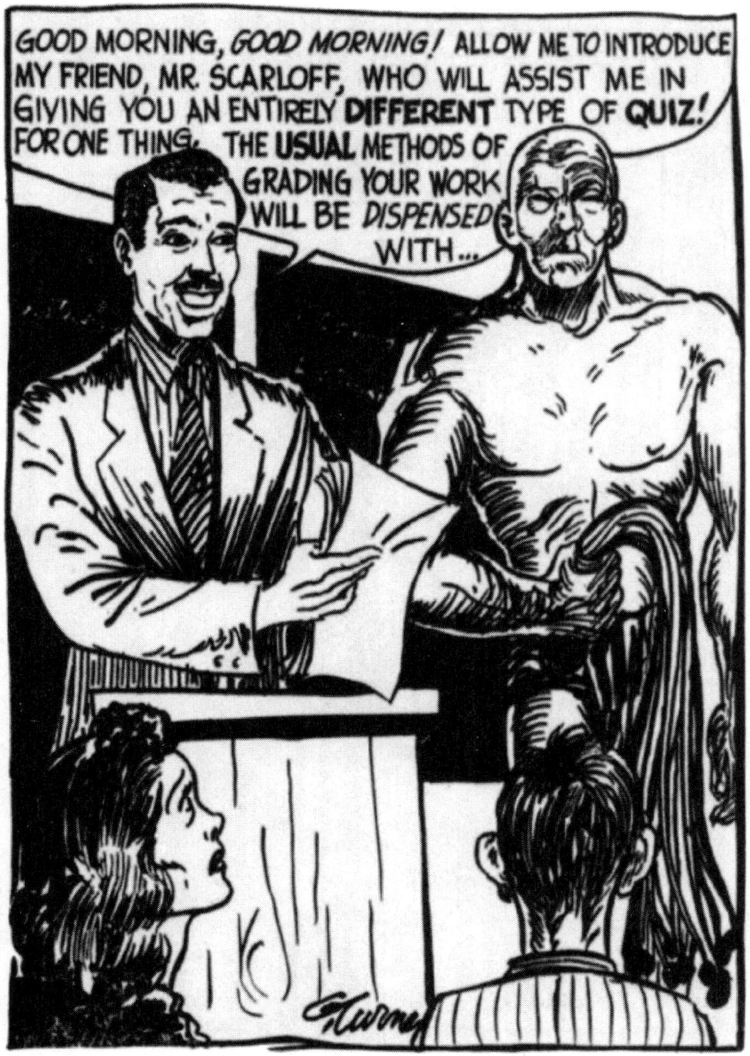
GOOD MORNING, GOOD MORNING! ALLOW ME TO INTRODUCE MY FRIEND, MR. SCARLOFF, WHO WILL ASSIST ME IN GIVING YOU AN ENTIRELY DIFFERENT TYPE OF QUIZ! FOR ONE THING, THE USUAL METHODS OF GRADING YOUR WORK WILL BE DISPENSED WITH...
Turner

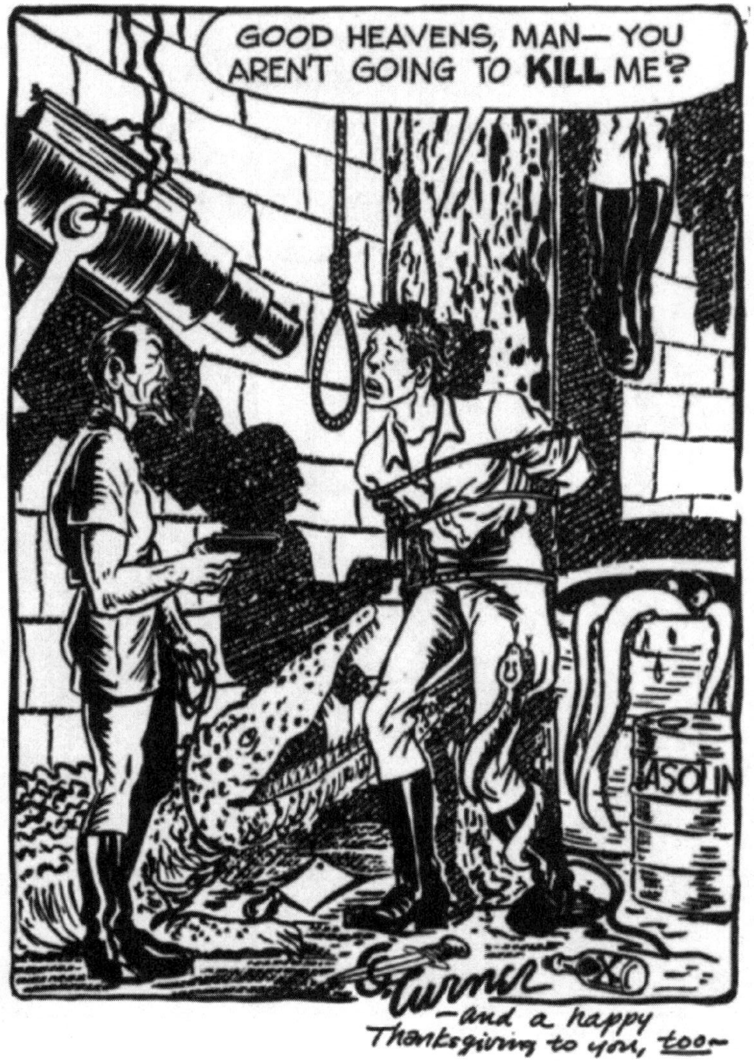
GOOD HEAVENS, MAN— YOU AREN'T GOING TO KILL ME?
ASOLIN
Turner
—and a happy Thanksgiving to you, too—

OH BILL! IT'S SO *FINE*! JUST LIKE CHOPIN'S POLONAISE—ONLY MUCH BETTER!

(The amateur composer's girl-friend being helped — Leap Year tactics, natch.)

TODAY'S DISTINGUISHED SPEAKER REALLY NEEDS NO INTRODUCTION... HE IS A WELL-KNOWN SORCERER AND VAMPIRE

George Turner said this campus-newspaper cartoon inspired a backlash of mock-epic proportions from the Faculty Council, which was duly appalled at the suggestion that cheating might be a classroom routine. So what else is new?

Though Styles May Change, Cartoonist's Sales Add Up

By PATSY DINAN
Globe-Times Staff Writer

Gahan's humor runs to the macabre, his friends say.

And a glance at his cartoons in the Aug. 7 Look and the July 23 Sports Illustrated backs up that analysis.

But Gahan Wilson doesn't go for having his cartoons "typed." He won't settle for a simplified tag to his style because his style is changing.

"My style has already changed once and it's going through another change now," he said, during his Amarillo visit with Mr. and Mrs. George Turner, 116 N. LaSalle.

Whatever this style is, it's selling. And Gahan has been trying the cartooning business for only three years.

This is not to say that he hasn't been thinking in terms of a cartooning career for a long time. There've been years for study and time at Amarillo Air Force Base to delay this 26-year-old in launching his profession.

"I never had to figure out what I wanted to be. I guess I'm lucky. I always wanted to be a cartoonist. I want to be a writer, too. In fact, I think I'm basically a writer more than anything else," Gahan says.

He was drawing comic strips at kindergarten age, before he could write.

A native of Evanston, Ill., he attended Evanston High School and the Todd School for Boys in Woodstock, Ill. Next he went to the Art Institute of Chicago. That's where he met Turner, his host here, who is an artist with Russell's Stationery.

After being graduated from the Chicago Art Institute, Gahan studied at the Academie Julien in Paris — serious art.

Although he says, "I haven't done any serious painting since Paris," he believes that "a cartoonist must know art — definitely."

"A cartoonist must study figure drawing and the like to have something to base his cartooning on," Gahan adds.

The tousled haired left-hander, whose Gaelic name means "rocky field," lives in New York so he can be his own "errand boy" in delivering cartoons to magazine art editors.

"Wednesday is the traditional market day for cartoons at all national magazines — and no editor knows just why — I've asked 'em," he says.

Each Wednesday Gahan submit's a week's work in rough form. The next Wednesday he picks them up. The "roughs" that have been okayed he finishes. The ones that have been rejected he submits to other magazines.

—Globe-Times Staff Photo

CARTOONIST GAHAN WILSON

Otherwise, he has no regular hours.

"I have no hours and no special office. A cartoonist can work anywhere so long as he can get to a mailbox," Gahan says.

"Quite a few cartoonists have broken in from places outside New York. Anybody who wants to be a cartoonist can do it through the mail because editors do look through their mail. They are always looking for something to buy — no matter where the cartoonist lives," Wilson adds.

"There's a man in Holland, Ton Smits, who has been selling major markets. You may have seen his stuff in the New Yorker," Gahan continues.

Asked for advice to hopeful cartoonists, Wilson says, "Try to sell the small markets first — usually everybody tries for the New Yorker. And the struggling cartoonist should take heart. It's slow, laborious work drawing an idea and trying to sharpen it up to bring it into focus. But once you start to sell you can live anywhere and keep any hours you want."

Gahan's hours start at about 5:30 a.m. because he feels that he works best in the early morning. Still there's not much routine to his work.

"I walk around the city, sit at my desk, go to museums — sweating out ideas," he says.

"I try to do ten roughs a week. If I get ahead I save 'em until the next week," he adds.

But he doesn't get his ideas for the sketches from gag-writers although he gets about two batches of gags a day from free-lance hopefuls who send unsolicited ideas for cartoons to artists whose work appears in national magazines.

And a number of Wilson's cartoons have no caption-lines — but not all of them," he says.

Although Gahan claims he's not strictly a ghoulish-type cartoonist, his reading tends toward weird fantasies.

Topping his list of favorite writers is Edgar Allan Poe.

And one of his objectives during his visit in Texas is "to see some good horror movies at the dialogue."

A *Globe-Times* clipping from 1952, noting a visit from George Turner's fellow alumnus of the Art Institute of Chicago, Gahan Wilson. Wilson's greater fortunes as a mass-market cartoonist lay yet ahead. First, Wilson experienced the indignity of finding several submissions to *The New Yorker* rejected but then resurrected in published cartoons by Charles Addams. (The obscured word in the opening paragraph is "macabre." And yes, the final paragraph is garbled beyond interpretation.)

George Turner's illustration for a 1952 reprinting of Matthew Gregory Lewis' narrative poem of 1799, "Courteous King Jamie," as published in a fanzine bearing the awkward title of *FaNews*.

George Turner's portrait of Boris Karloff, as seen in 1939's *Son of Frankenstein*. The faded handwriting (at bottom) is an appreciative note: "To George Turner— with sincere congratulations on a magnificent piece of work. [*Signed*] Boris Karloff." The ink-on-scratchboard brush drawing dates from circa 1960. George seldom displayed his own work, but this item was an exception; framed alongside the actor's note, it hung in George's Texas and Hollywood offices for many years.

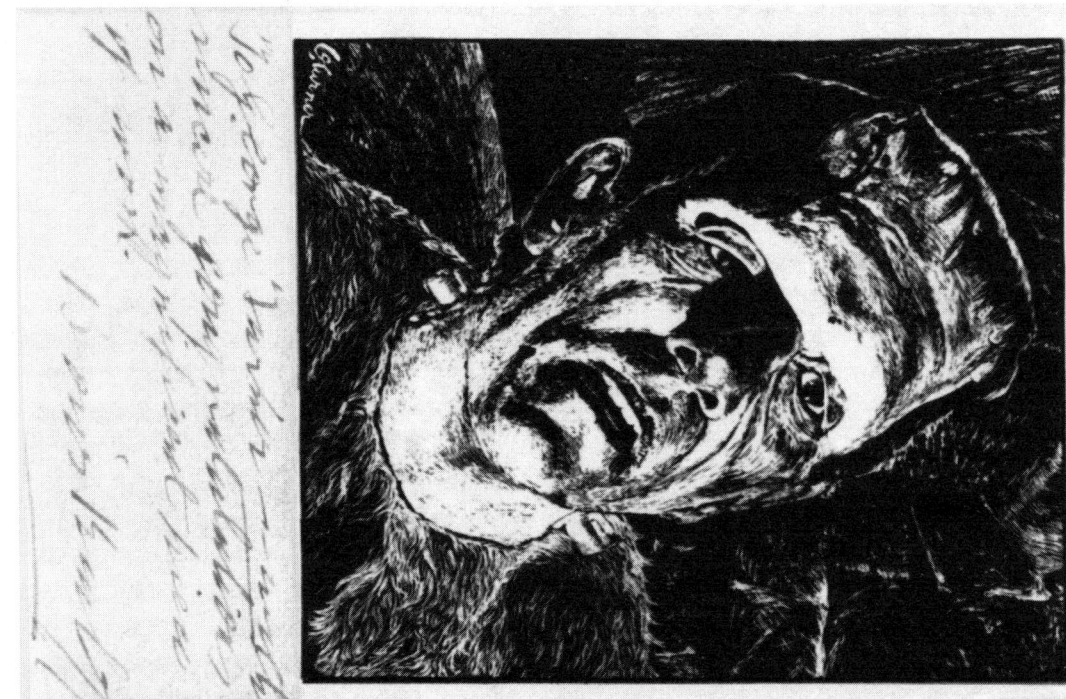

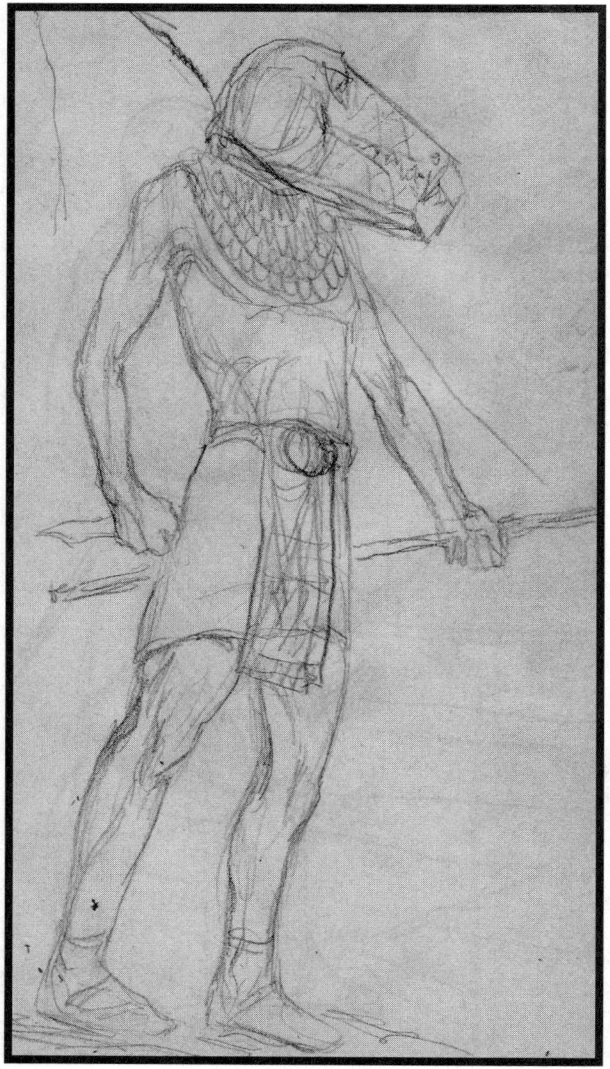

The images seen here come from a file of conceptual sketches for an abandoned project that George had called *The Great Adventure*. Elements thereof found their way into George's 1966 comic serial, *Tarzan and the Crocodile God*, as published in *The Burroughs Bulletin*.

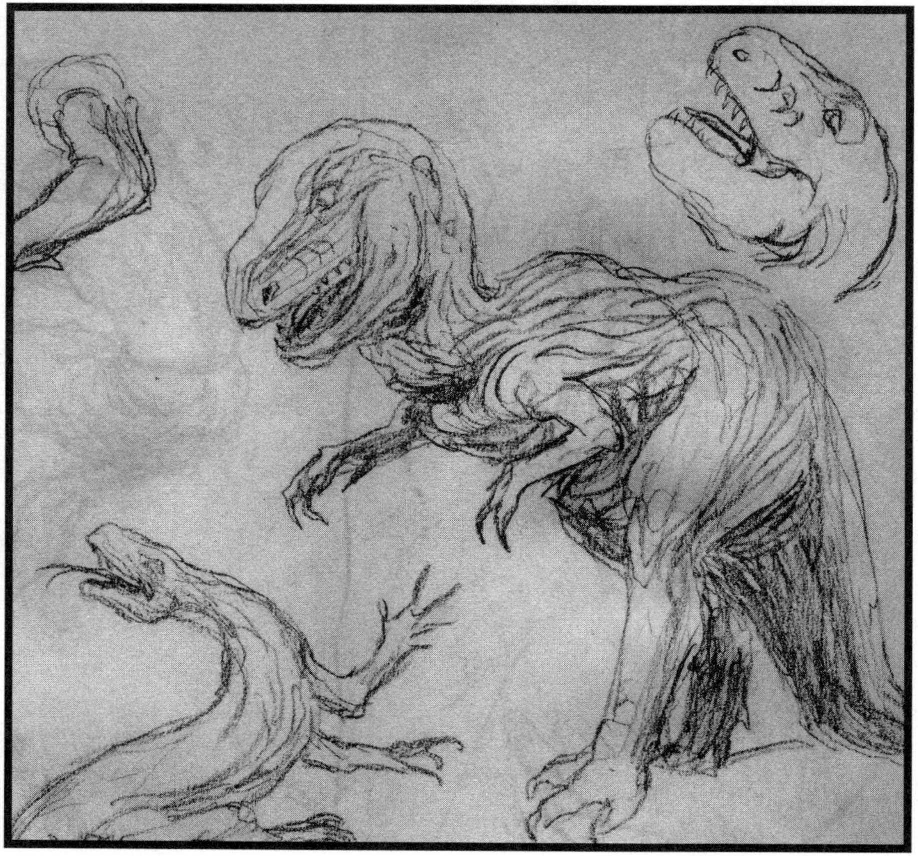

And speaking of Tarzan: George later reworked his tale of *Tarzan & the Crocodile God* into a set of newspaper-syndicate samples when the writer-illustrator job on the daily *Tarzan* feature came open. George did not land the assignment, but these tryouts (hitherto unpublished) placed him among the finalists.

OPAR, LYING IN RUINS FOR COUNTLESS CENTURIES ...RULED BY THE HIDEOUS BEAST-MEN, WHO HAVE LONG FORGOTTEN THE CIVILIZATION THAT BUILT IT...

GOLDEN-HAIRED QUEEN RUA LIVES WITHIN THE TEMPLE, A PRISONER OF HER OWN SUBJECTS...

KROG! WHAT ARE YOU DOING IN THE TEMPLE?

I CANNOT BEAR YOUR UNHAPPINESS ANY LONGER, YOUR HIGHNESS — I WANT TO HELP YOU!

NOBODY CAN HELP ME. YOU MUST GO BEFORE YOU ARE DISCOVERED.

PLEASE HEAR ME OUT, QUEEN RUA! I CAN GET YOU AWAY FROM OOPAR TO FREEDOM!

I WONDER ABOUT QUEEN RUA. POOR, BEAUTIFUL THING... HAPPINESS ALWAYS ELUDED HER.

HOURS LATER...

FREE! FREE AT LAST!

ESCAPE? HOW?

THERE IS A SECRET PASSAGE —I FOUND IT LONG AGO. PLEASE FOLLOW, O QUEEN.

THAT SCREAM— A WOMAN!

KEEP AWAY OR I'LL—

WAIT, KROG —I SAW SOMETHING OUT THERE...

Of course, the generic jungle-dwelling man thus depicted is not Tarzan until Tarzan's trademark-wranglers buy into the tale. In this light, George retooled his original script into various forms over the years, featuring other heroic characters in other settings conducive to robust adventure.

A C K N O W L E D G M E N T S

Design & Cover Painting: CREMO STUDIOS, INCORPORATED

Cover-design Elements: BEN SARGENT and SARGENT BROTHERS PRINT SHOP of Austin

Technical Assistance: JULIE KING, NATHAN RICH, and *The Business Press* of Fort Worth

Research Assistance: The GLOBE-NEWS REFERENCE LIBRARY of Amarillo, Texas, and the JAMES P. CORNETTE MEMORIAL LIBRARY, West Texas A&M University at Canyon

Crucial Kibitzing: D. LEE THOMAS, JR., ANDREW VOGEL, RICHARD L. CONNOR, LARRY D. SPRINGER, J. KERRY PRICE, STEPHEN R. BISSETTE, GREG JACKSON, MARK MARTIN, JOHN WOOLEY, WELDON ADAMS, ART LARA, and DENNIS SPIES

Portions of this collection have appeared in markedly different form in the *Sunday News-Globe* of Amarillo, Texas; *Amateur Art & Camera* magazine; *The Prairie* of West Texas State College (West Texas A&M University); *FaNews* magazine; the Nortex Press edition of *Murder in the Palo Duro & Other Panhandle Mysteries*; the Luminary Press edition of *Spawn of Skull Island*; and publications of *The Business Press* of Fort Worth.

The "Sharktopus" drawing (page 35) appears by permission of illustrator Mark Evan Walker and is Copyright © 2005 by M.H. Price & M.E. Walker. The lyrical excerpt from Greg Jackson's "Grandma's Front Porch" (page 64) appears by permission and is Copyright © 2005 by the composer and Liquid Lady Publishing, B.M.I. References to *King Kong* acknowledge the Trademark ™ of Warner Bros. Studios, Incorporated. References to *Frankenstein* acknowledge the Trademark ™ of Universal Pictures Corporation. References to *Tarzan* acknowledge the Trademark ™ of Edgar Rice Burroughs, Incorporated.